Corporate Governance in Latvia

OECD
BETTER POLICIES FOR BETTER LIVES

This work is published under the responsibility of the Secretary-General of the OECD. The opinions expressed and arguments employed herein do not necessarily reflect the official views of OECD member countries.

This document and any map included herein are without prejudice to the status of or sovereignty over any territory, to the delimitation of international frontiers and boundaries and to the name of any territory, city or area.

Please cite this publication as:
OECD (2017), *Corporate Governance in Latvia*, OECD Publishing, Paris.
http://dx.doi.org/10.1787/9789264268180-en

ISBN 978-92-64-26817-3 (print)
ISBN 978-92-64-26818-0 (PDF)

Series: Corporate Governance
ISSN 2077-6527 (print)
ISSN 2077-6535 (online)

Revised version, April 2017.
Details of revisions available at: *http://www.oecd.org/about/publishing/Corrigendum-CorporateGovernanceLatvia.pdf*

Corrigenda to OECD publications may be found on line at: *www.oecd.org/about/publishing/corrigenda.htm*.

Foreword

Since regaining its independence in 1991, Latvia has made great strides, becoming one of the fastest-growing economies in Europe in recent years. Over this same period, Latvia's government has taken significant steps to improve the framework for the corporate governance of listed and state-owned enterprises (SOEs). Continuing to improve this framework is an important part of ensuring Latvia remains on a path of sustainable economic development. This review includes key recommendations in this regard that, if implemented, could support a deepening of Latvia's capital markets and increase the transparency and efficiency of its economically and politically important SOE sector.

This *Corporate Governance Accession Review of Latvia* was prepared by the OECD Secretariat to support the review of Latvia undertaken by the OECD Corporate Governance Committee and the OECD Working Party on State Ownership and Privatisation Practices as part of the process of Latvia's accession to the OECD (see the Roadmap for the Accession of Latvia to the OECD Convention), which was launched in May 2013, when the OECD Council decided to open accession discussions with Latvia. This process included a requirement to assess Latvia's willingness and ability to implement the substantive OECD legal instruments in the field of corporate governance, namely the *Recommendation of the Council on Principles of Corporate Governance* ("the Principles") and the *Recommendation of the Council on Guidelines on Corporate Governance of State-Owned Enterprises* ("the Guidelines"), and to evaluate its policies and practices as compared to OECD best policies and practices in this area.

The report that follows provides the results of this assessment. It finds that Latvia's framework for the corporate governance of listed companies is largely consistent with the Principles. The practical reality, however, is that Latvia's capital market is small. Further strengthening the corporate governance framework could help to deepen the market and attract investment. Recommendations include: improving the enforcement of, and sanctions for, rules against market misconduct; strengthening the efficiency of judicial review of commercial cases; reviewing the impact of Latvia's insolvency framework; and clarifying the role and composition of companies' audit committees. The report includes, in particular, a recommendation to address weaknesses identified in the framework for the treatment and disclosure of related party transactions.

The picture with respect to SOE corporate governance is more complex because, as this review was undertaken, the government was in the early stages of implementing major SOE reforms. If implemented effectively, these reforms would address many of the weaknesses identified by the OECD review. Significantly, the reforms – including a new SOE corporate governance law – have resulted in the establishment of a state enterprise ownership coordination function, and launched a process to re-establish boards of directors (which had been abolished in 2009) in Latvia's large, commercially-oriented SOEs. Other reforms underway include requirements to clarify SOE commercial and non-commercial objectives and strategies, and to enhance disclosure and reporting.

Latvia acceded to the OECD Convention and thus became an OECD Member on 1 July 2016. The information in this report is current through July 2016, following exchanges with the Latvian authorities in early August 2016. The report was prepared by Mary Crane-Charef under the oversight of Daniel Blume of the OECD Directorate for Financial and Enterprise Affairs.

Table of contents

Abbreviations and acronyms 7

Executive summary 9

Chapter 1. Introduction to the corporate governance review of Latvia 13

Notes 15
References 16

Chapter 2. Latvia's corporate governance landscape 17

2.1 Corporate Ownership, Structure and Control 20
2.2 The Corporate Governance Framework 26
2.3 Overview of the SOE Sector 44
2.4 The Legal and Regulatory Framework for SOEs 46
Notes 52
References 58

Chapter 3. Latvia and the core Corporate Governance Principles: The Roadmap for Accession 61

3.1 Ensuring a consistent regulatory framework that provides for the existence and effective enforcement of shareholder rights and the equitable treatment of shareholders, including minority and foreign shareholders. 62
3.2 Requiring timely and reliable disclosure of corporate information in accordance with internationally recognised standards of accounting, auditing and non-financial reporting 74
3.3 Establishing effective separation of the government's role as an owner of state-owned companies and the government's role as regulator, particularly with regard to market regulation. 89
3.4 Ensuring a level playing field in markets where state-owned enterprises and private sector companies compete in order to avoid market distortions. 97
3.5 Recognising stakeholder rights as established by law or through mutual agreements and the duties, rights and responsibilities of corporate supervisory boards. 99
Notes 109
References 117

Chapter 4. Conclusions and recommendations for Latvia's corporate governance framework.... 121

4.1 Conclusions 122
4.2 Recommendations 124
References 126

Annex A. Latvian state-owned enterprises 127

Tables

2.1 Key economic indicators, 2010-15 18
2.2 Structure of the Latvian economy (by value added, %) 19
2.3 Market capitalization of the ten most-traded Latvian companies, 1 January – 31 December 2015 22
2.4 Securities traded on Nasdaq Riga (as of 31 December 2015) 23
2.5 Nasdaq Baltic recommendations targeting issuers and investors to increase IPOs in Baltic markets 24
2.6 Company compliance rates with the Nasdaq Principles of Corporate Governance as of 2013 43
2.7 An overview of the companies majority-owned by the Latvian government 46
2.8 SOEs that may establish supervisory boards 48
3.1 Application of IFRS by large SOEs (as per the PPCSCL size threshold) 77
3.2 Sanctions Applied by LASA for violations of audit standards 79
3.3 Line ministry websites disclosing state enterprise shareholding information 86
3.4 Line ministries' enterprise ownership assessments under the PPCSCL, as of January 2016 91
3.5 Status of guidelines and regulations prepared by the Coordination Institution as of end-June 2016 95
3.6 Insolvency case statistics 102

Figures

2.1 OMX Riga Index Value, January 2000 to August 2015 21
2.2 Market capitalisation and turnover (EUR millions) 21
2.3 Number of listed companies and companies paying dividends 23
2.4 Share of SOEs of total dependent employment 45

Boxes

2.1 FCMC enforcement statistics under the FIML, 2009-15 35
2.2 Latvian Shipping Company and Ventspils Nafta 39
2.3 Main responsibilities of the Coordination Institution according to the Public Persons Enterprises and Capital Shares Governance Law 50
2.4 Latvia's state enterprise ownership rationale: Article 88.1, State Administration Structure Law 52
3.1 Preliminary proposals to amend the framework for reviewing, approving, and disclosing related party transactions 69
3.2 Financial reporting standards requirements under Latvian law 75
3.3 Provisions for the disclosure of related party transactions 88
3.4 Insolvency framework in practice: Liepajas Metalurgs 104

Abbreviations and acronyms

ADR	alternative dispute resolution
AGM	annual general meeting
AOA	articles of association
BICG	Baltic Institute for Corporate Governance
Committee	Corporate Governance Committee
CL	Commercial Law
CSCC	Cross-Sectoral Coordination Centre
EBRD	European Bank for Reconstruction and Development
EGM	extraordinary general meeting
EU	European Union
EUR	euro
FCMC	Financial and Capital Market Commission
FICIL	Foreign Investors Council in Latvia
FIML	Financial Instruments Markets Law
GAAP	Generally Accepted Accounting Principles
GCL	Group of Companies Law
GDP	gross domestic product
IFRS	International Financial Reporting Standards
IMF	International Monetary Fund
IPO	initial public offering
ISA	International Standards on Auditing
JSC	joint stock company
LASA	Latvian Association of Sworn Auditors
LCD	Latvian Central Depository
LGCSCC	Law on State and Local Government Capital Shares and Capital Companies
LLC	limited liability company
LMT	Latvijas Mobilais Telefons
LPA	Latvian Privatisation Agency
Nasdaq Riga	regulated market organiser

NCP	National Contact Point
OECD	Organisation for Economic Co-operation and Development
ORICGS	Central Storage of Regulated Information
PPCSCL	Public Persons Capital Shares and Companies Law
SASL	State Administration Structure Law
SME	small- and medium-sized enterprise
SOE	state-owned enterprise
UNCITRAL	UN Commission on International Trade Law
USD	U.S. dollar
Working Party	Working Party on State Ownership and Privatisation Practices

Executive summary

This report assesses Latvia's legal, regulatory and institutional framework for corporate governance and the country's implementation of the *G20/OECD Principles of Corporate Governance* ("the Principles") and the *OECD Guidelines on Corporate Governance of State-Owned Enterprises* ("the Guidelines"). It first examines the corporate governance landscape, then turns to the five "core corporate governance principles" set out in the *Roadmap for the Accession of Latvia to the OECD Convention.*

Corporate governance in Latvia

This report finds that Latvia's framework for the corporate governance of listed companies is largely consistent with the Principles. The practical reality, however, is that Latvia's capital market is small. Further strengthening the corporate governance framework could help to deepen the market and attract investment. Recommendations include: improving the enforcement of, and sanctions for, rules against market misconduct; strengthening the efficiency of judicial review of commercial cases; reviewing the impact of Latvia's insolvency framework; and clarifying the role and composition of companies' audit committees. This report includes, in particular, a recommendation to address weaknesses identified in the framework for the treatment and disclosure of related party transactions.

The picture with respect to SOE corporate governance is more complex because, as this review was undertaken, the government was in the early stages of implementing major SOE reforms. If implemented effectively, these reforms would address many of the weaknesses identified by the OECD review. Significantly, the reforms – including a new SOE corporate governance law – have resulted in the establishment of a state enterprise ownership co-ordination function and launched a process to re-establish boards of directors (abolished in 2009) in Latvia's large, commercially-oriented SOEs. Other reforms underway include requirements to clarify SOE commercial and non-commercial objectives and strategies, and to enhance disclosure and reporting.

Latvia and the core corporate governance principles

Ensuring the enforcement of shareholder rights and equitable treatment

Latvia's legal framework appears to broadly protect and facilitate the exercise of shareholder rights in accordance with the Principles. However, some cases of abuse of shareholder rights have been noted, including delays in responding to shareholder requests to schedule extraordinary general meetings and barriers raised to their participation, and instances where controlling shareholders failed to make mandatory share buyout offers to minority shareholders when they exceeded the 50% ownership threshold. The Latvian government is continuing concerted efforts to strengthen the judicial system and is taking concrete steps to address the challenge of enforcement against market abuse, including insider trading and abusive self-dealing.

Timely and reliable disclosure in accordance with international standards

Latvia's framework for listed companies generally meets the Principles' recommendations in this area. While International Financial Reporting Standards (IFRS) are required of only some listed companies, the requirement covers most of Latvia's most actively traded listed companies. Latvian SOEs have implemented most Guidelines recommendations on disclosure, but IFRS reporting remains an important concern. Going forward, the Latvian government is committed to implementing IFRS in its largest SOEs and to integrating additional information in future annual aggregate reports of Latvia's Co-ordination Institution. The requirements to disclose governance, ownership and voting structures for both listed and state-owned companies are generally consistent with the Principles and the Guidelines recommendations.

Effective separation of the government's role as owner and its regulatory role

This assessment of the effective separation of the Latvian government's role as both owner and regulator of SOEs comes with a caveat: Latvia's overall framework for SOE governance has just been reformed. In early 2016, a number of key provisions from the Public Persons Capital Shares and Companies Law (PPCSCL), had just entered into force. Going forward, the Latvian government will continue to work on effective implementation of the PPCSCL, supported by the recent amendments to the state enterprise ownership rationale in the State Administration Structure Law. Latvia could also consider: establishing professional supervisory boards in all large, commercially oriented SOEs; ensuring that the Co-ordination Institution has the resources it needs; and improving current practices for expressing the state's rationale for enterprise ownership, both at the government-wide level and for specific SOEs.

Ensuring a level playing field

According to the Latvian authorities, SOEs do not receive any preferential treatment, including access to debt and equity finance (though there is a question as to whether some strategic SOEs enjoy implicit guarantees). There is also no evidence that SOE stakeholders face significant obstacles when seeking redress, though – as in the private sector – court efficiency and the availability of quality alternative dispute resolution mechanisms are challenges. Latvia's framework governing SOEs and public procurement appears in line with OECD recommendations. Latvia has also recognised the need to strengthen its framework in regard to practices for identifying and disclosing public policy objectives and related costs. Latvia plans to require the Co-ordination Institution to work with line ministries and SOEs to publish information regarding public policy objectives, their associated costs, and their achievements.

Recognising stakeholder rights and the duties, rights and responsibilities of boards

Latvia's stakeholder rights framework generally reflects OECD recommendations. Some large Latvian SOEs also voluntarily disclose information on stakeholder relations. Latvia does not, however, have a strong tradition of formal mechanisms to ensure the participation of employees and other stakeholders in corporate governance processes. Latvia's ongoing efforts in this area include improving the efficiency of the courts and the availability and quality of alternative dispute resolution measures and reviewing and strengthening whistle-blower reporting channels and protections. Latvia should continue its work to facilitate stakeholders' ability to communicate their concerns about illegal or unethical practices, with such protections included in internal controls, ethics and compliance programmes. Questions remain regarding the implementation of Latvia's 2010 insolvency framework, although the government has made some progress addressing the low insolvency clearance rates. The government's development of and commitment to a long-term insolvency policy – coupled with active enforcement and improvement targets – is key to restoring confidence in the framework. With respect to boards of listed companies, Latvia's two-tiered board structure generally follows most OECD recommendations related to the duties, rights and responsibilities of supervisory boards, including in relation to stakeholders. For SOEs, Latvia's government has committed to re-establishing professional boards by ensuring the application of the PPCSCL and by implementing regulations and guidance on SOE supervisory boards, including board nomination criteria and procedures, and by establishing boards in 12 large commercially oriented SOEs.

Chapter 1

Introduction to the corporate governance review of Latvia

The Review of Corporate Governance in Latvia was prepared as part of the process of Latvia's accession to OECD Membership. The report describes the corporate governance setting for both listed companies and the state-owned sector (SOEs). The Review then examines the legal and regulatory framework and company practices to assess the degree to which the recommendations of the G20/OECD Principles of Corporate Governance and the OECD Guidelines on Corporate Governance of State-Owned Enterprises have been implemented.

As part of Latvia's accession process to the OECD, this report reviews Latvia's implementation of the *Recommendation of the Council on Principles of Corporate Governance*[1] (the Principles) and the *Recommendation of the Council on Guidelines on Corporate Governance of State-Owned Enterprises*[2] (the Guidelines). It is aimed at supporting the assessment of Latvia's willingness and ability to implement the substantive OECD legal instruments in the field of corporate governance, and an evaluation of its policies and practices as compared to OECD best policies and practices in this area. In this regard, it reviews Latvia's legal, regulatory and institutional framework and implementation with respect to five "core corporate governance principles" set out in the OECD's *Roadmap for the Accession of Latvia to the OECD Convention* ("the Roadmap"). These five core principles are as follows:

- Ensuring a consistent regulatory framework that provides for the existence and effective enforcement of shareholder rights and the equitable treatment of shareholders, including minority and foreign shareholders;
- Requiring timely and reliable disclosure of corporate information in accordance with internationally recognised standards of accounting, auditing and non-financial reporting;
- Establishing effective separation of the government's role as an owner of state-owned companies and the government's role as regulator, particularly with regard to market regulation;
- Ensuring a level playing field in markets where state-owned enterprises and private sector companies compete in order to avoid market distortions;
- Recognising stakeholder rights as established by law or through mutual agreements and the duties, rights and responsibilities of corporate boards of directors.

This report is guided by the document titled "Concepts to Guide Corporate Governance Accession Reviews"[3] (the "Concept Paper"). The Concept Paper provides a methodology for conducting accession examinations, identifying which Principles and Guidelines recommendations are most relevant for assessing accession candidate countries against the five Roadmap principles. It integrates and updates (1) a 2014 assessment by the OECD's Corporate Governance Committee ("Committee") of Latvia's corporate governance framework vis-à-vis the Principles and (2) a 2014 assessment by the OECD's Working Party on State Ownership and Privatisation Practices ("the Working Party") of Latvia's SOE sector relative to the SOE Guidelines.[4] Both assessments contained substantial recommendations to strengthen Latvia's corporate governance framework for listed and state-controlled entities, which were communicated to the Latvian government in letters from the chairs of the Committee and the Working Party in November 2014 and January 2015, respectively.[5]

The information included in this report also draws upon a detailed self-assessment by the Latvian authorities against all of the Principles, prepared with reference to the *OECD Methodology for Implementation of the Corporate Governance Principles*[6] and submitted to the OECD Secretariat in 2014 as part of Latvia's review under the Principles, as well as responses to a standard questionnaire on the SOE Guidelines submitted in 2014 as part of the Working Party assessment. The report further draws upon (1) Latvia's responses to the aforementioned recommendations made by the Committee and the Working Party following the 2014 assessments and (2) a response to a joint letter dated 9 December

2015 from the Committee and Working Party chairs with recommendations following an initial review of this report by the Working Party on 28 October 2015 and by the Committee on 19 November. It includes, also, Latvia's responses to a series of supplementary follow-up questions, as well as missions organized in Riga in February 2014, May 2014, June 2014, September 2015 and January 2016 with public officials, market participants, academics and other experts. Secretariat fact-finding missions, interviews with public officials, market participants, academics and relevant literature have also served as input to this corporate governance assessment of Latvia.

It must also be noted that the accession review process for Latvia was initiated in parallel with the Working Party and Committee reviews of the Guidelines and the Principles prior to these documents' adoption on 8 July 2015; representatives of Latvia participated in the reviews of both instruments as an Associate in the Working Party and Committee. While this report does not provide a comprehensive assessment of how Latvia is implementing each of the revisions to the Guidelines and Principles, the updated Concept Paper serving as a reference for this report takes into account the revisions to these instruments and provides updated references to those Guidelines and Principles recommendations that are most relevant to assessing candidate countries against the five core corporate governance principles set out in the *Roadmap for the Accession of Latvia to the OECD Convention*. References to revised Guidelines and Principles recommendations have been integrated as relevant in this report.

This report is structured to provide, first, an executive summary containing overall conclusions with respect to the five "core corporate governance principles" set out in the Roadmap. These conclusions are based on the assessment provided in subsequent sections of this report, including an overview of Latvia's corporate governance landscape (Chapter 2), followed by a detailed review of Latvia's performance against each of the five Roadmap core principles (Chapter 3). Finally, Chapter 4 provides (1) the conclusions of assessments made by the OECD Corporate Governance Committee and the OECD Working Party on State Ownership and Privatisation Practice's position relative to the Principles and the Guidelines, respectively; and (2) a set of recommendations by which Latvia may further align its framework with these instruments.

Notes

1. See online here: www.oecd.org/daf/ca/principles-corporate-governance.htm
2. See online here: www.oecd.org/daf/ca/guidelines-corporate-governance-soes.htm
3. First issued in 2008, this unpublished concept paper has been updated to take into account the 8 July 2015 adoption of the Principles and the Guidelines. It takes as a main reference the *Roadmap for the Accession of Latvia to the OECD Convention* as well as similar roadmaps developed for Colombia, Lithuania and Costa Rica, which set out the terms, conditions and processes for their accession.
4. The Working Party assessment was prepared in response to a request from the Latvian government made prior to the launching of the accession process with Latvia. While separate from the process of Latvia's accession to the OECD, the Working Party assessment provides a useful reference for this report. The review is available to download (PDF) from www.oecd.org/daf/ca/oecd-review-corporate-governance-soe-latvia.htm.

5. The Committee's 2014 assessment and its recommendations were based on the 2004 edition of the Principles, which were updated in 2015. For the text of the 2004 Principles, see online here: *www.oecd.org/daf/ca/oecd-principles-corporate-governance-2004.htm*. Similarly, the Working Party's assessment was based on the 2005 edition of the Guidelines, which were also updated in 2015. For the text of the 2005 Guidelines, see online here: *www.oecd.org/daf/ca/oecd-guidelines-corporate-governance-soes-2005.htm*.

6. See online here: *www.oecd.org/daf/ca/corporategovernanceprinciples/37776417.pdf*. Note: The Methodology was under review at the time of publication to reflect the updated 2015 Principles.

References

OECD (2015a), *G20/OECD Principles of Corporate Governance*, OECD Publishing, Paris. *http://dx.doi.org/10.1787/9789264236882-en*.

OECD (2015b), *OECD Guidelines on Corporate Governance of State-Owned Enterprises*, 2015 Edition, OECD Publishing, Paris, http://dx.doi.org/10.1787/9789264244160-en .

OECD (2015c), *Recommendation of the Council on Principles of Corporate Governance*, *http://acts.oecd.org/Instruments/ShowInstrumentView.aspx?InstrumentID=322&InstrumentPID=358&Lang=en&Book=False*.

OECD (2015d), *Recommendation of the Council on Guidelines on Corporate Governance of State-Owned Enterprises*, *http://acts.oecd.org/Instruments/ShowInstrumentView.aspx?InstrumentID=323&InstrumentPID=359&Lang=en&Book=False*.

OECD (2015e), *OECD Review of the Corporate Governance of State-Owned Enterprises in Latvia*, *www.oecd.org/daf/ca/oecd-review-corporate-governance-soe-latvia.htm.*

OECD (2013), *Roadmap for the Accession of Latvia to the OECD Convention*, *www.oecd.org/officialdocuments/publicdisplaydocumentpdf/?cote=C(2013)122/FINAL&docLanguage=En*

Chapter 2

Latvia's corporate governance landscape

This chapter describes Latvia's corporate governance framework for listed and state-owned enterprises (SOE), within the context of the country's recent economic history and current business environment. It has four parts:

1. ***Corporate ownership, structure and control**, including (1) corporate ownership, listing trends, and recommendations for deepening Latvia's capital markets; (2) the role of institutional investors, and (3) the role and responsibility of companies' supervisory boards;*
2. *The **corporate governance** framework itself, as informed by the overall legal, regulatory, policy and institutional frameworks;*
3. *An overview of the **SOE** sector;*
4. *The **legal and regulatory framework for SOEs**, including the Public Persons Capital Shares and Companies Law (PPCSCL) and the State Administration Structure Law, including a discussion of the reintroduction of SOE supervisory boards and the establishment of a new Coordination Institution.*

Latvia, a country of 2 million people that regained its independence in 1991, has experienced periods of both rapid growth and severe economic crisis. This chapter describes how Latvia's recent economic history has greatly affected the development of the country's corporate governance framework for listed and state-controlled entities.

Economy. Following its entry into the European Union in 2004, Latvia's annual growth accelerated to more than 10% per year between 2005 and 2007. This growth was subsequently seen as unsustainable, fuelled by a real estate bubble and excessive credit. By 2008, as global liquidity tightened, capital flows came to a sudden stop. Uncertainty regarding the largest domestically-owned bank led to a run on its deposits and a system-wide liquidity shortage. The result was a 4% drop in GDP in 2008 and further 18% reduction in 2009, the most severe contraction in Europe, leading the Latvian government to request financial assistance from the IMF and European Commission. However, following the adoption of strict austerity measures, the economy has resumed growth since 2011, becoming the fastest-growing economy in the EU in 2013, just prior to adopting the euro in January 2014. While observers including European Commission had projected continuing annual GDP growth of above 4% for 2014-15, more recent estimates – including those provided by the government of Latvia – indicate a slowdown to 2.4% in 2014 and 2.1% in 2015.

Table 2.1 **Key economic indicators, 2010-15**

	2010	2011	2012	2013	2014	2015[1]
Indicator	*Increase over the previous year (%)*					
GDP	-2.9	5.0	4.8	4.2	2.4	2.1
Consumer prices	-1.1	4.4	2.3	0.0	0.6	0.8
	As a percentage					
Unemployment	19.5	16.2	15.0	11.9	10.8	9.7
	As a percentage of gross domestic product					
Gross public debt	46.8	42.7	40.9	38.2	40.0	37.0
Export-import balance	-1.5	-5.0	-4.4	-2.9	-2.9	-1.8

1. Forecasted.

Source: Latvia Ministry of Economics, Economic Development of Latvia, June 2015. See online here: https://www.em.gov.lv/files/tautsaimniecibas_attistiba/zin/2015_jun_eng.pdf

The Latvian Ministry of Economics credits the country's post-crisis recovery in part to an increase in Latvian exports: Overall exports of goods and services exceeded pre-crisis levels by 25%. In 2014, 73% of Latvian exports went to the European Union, while 15% went to the Commonwealth of Independent States. Latvia adopted the euro beginning in January 2014. However, developments in the Russian Federation (hereinafter "Russia") and Ukraine present downside risks to Latvia's growing economy, according to 2014 assessments made by the European Commission, the IMF, the Latvian government and OECD.[1] Additionally, Latvia's economy could be negatively affected by prolonged weakness in euro-area trade-partner countries.

Table 2.2 **Structure of the Latvian economy (by value added, %)**

	2000	2005	2009	2011	2012	2013	2014
Agriculture and forestry	5.2	4.3	3.7	3.9	3.7	3.6	3.4
Manufacturing	15.7	13.2	10.9	13.1	12.9	12.6	12.2
Other industry	4.3	3.2	5.2	5.0	4.7	4.4	4.2
Construction	6.4	6.4	7.4	5.4	6.1	6.4	6.7
Trade and accommodation	15.2	17.8	16.4	16.3	15.7	15.8	15.7
Transport and storage	11.8	12.3	10.3	10.2	10.3	9.7	9.6
Other commercial services	24.0	27.5	29.0	30.4	31.3	32.7	33.2
Public services	17.4	15.2	17.2	15.6	15.2	14.8	15.1
Total	**100**	**100**	**100**	**100**	**100**	**100**	**100**

Source: Ibid.

Business environment and capital markets. The vast majority of Latvian enterprises are micro, small and medium-sized companies. The State Revenue Service reports that 270 or 0.2% of Latvia's companies are characterised as large enterprises. The most popular legal form for entrepreneurship is a private limited liability company (90.35%). Approximately 950 companies, or 0.65% of all registered companies, are registered as public limited liability companies (also referred to as joint-stock companies), allowing for the public trade of shares.

The capital market in Latvia, as in the entire Baltic region, is small. Companies issuing equity or debt in Latvia do so via the Nasdaq Riga exchange. (The NASDAQ stock exchange in Latvia, along with the exchanges in Tallinn and Vilnius, form the Baltic Market; the NASDAQ exchange and ownership structure of listed companies are described more fully in section 2.1.) As of January 2016, 26 public limited liability companies were listed on the Nasdaq Riga exchange. Seventy share issues were registered with the Latvian Central Depository, including 26 securities issues that are in public circulation and 44 securities issues that are not in public circulation. Four companies are listed on the exchange's first tier, or Main List, which requires issuers to have market capitalisation of at least EUR 4 million and free float value exceeding EUR 10 million, or 25% of shares. Twenty-one companies are listed on the second tier, or Secondary List, which does not have quantitative requirements for issuers and shares issued by them. A further 14 companies have issued debt via the Nasdaq Riga bond list. Main, secondary, and bond list companies generally must follow the same requirements under the Financial Instruments Market Law (FIML), Commercial Law (CL) and Nasdaq Riga listing requirements. The only major difference is that Main and bond list companies must follow International Financial Reporting Standards (IFRS).[2] Companies issuing debt are also subject to less frequent financial reporting requirements. First North – a NASDAQ OMX Baltic alternative market segment with less stringent requirements for disclosure than the main, secondary and bond lists – was launched in 2007. Since then, three companies have traded on the First North Riga market, though as of January 2016 there was only one. As of 2015, corporate bonds can also be admitted to trading on First North Baltic market.

State-owned enterprises play an important role in the economy; many of Latvia's largest companies are SOEs. (See also section 2.3.) An annual "Top 101" report prepared by the Prudentia investment company in collaboration with Nasdaq Riga concluded that five of Latvia's ten most valuable companies are SOEs.[3] By comparison, only three listed companies – Olainfarm, Ventspils Nafta and Latvijas Gaze – made it into the top ten, and only seven listed companies made it into the top 101, an indication of the small role played by the capital market for most Latvian corporate finance.

2.1. Corporate Ownership, Structure and Control

Latvia has struggled to develop an active capital market since 1995, when its Stock Exchange first began trading. Even taking into account the small size of its economy,[4] both the value and volume of trading in Latvia's equity market are quite low. Latvia's total market capitalisation of EUR 842 million as of December 2012 was 3.9% of GDP in comparison to the OECD average of 75%, while trading volume as a percentage of GDP was even lower – 0.1% compared to the OECD average of 70%, according to World Bank indicators.[5]

Corporate ownership, listing trends and recommendations for deepening Latvia's capital markets

Latvia's listed companies are characterised by concentrated ownership and low liquidity. Only eight listed companies had more than 1 000 trades of their shares over the course of 2015.[6] Domestic share ownership across the Baltics, including in Latvia, is concentrated among a few large strategic investors, with a small base of medium-sized investors and a wide range of micro-investors. An April 2015 Nasdaq Baltic study on how to deepen Baltic capital markets explains that the weak retail investment culture and resulting concentrated ownership in Baltic markets, including Latvia's, are due to a number of reasons. These include "negative experiences during economic and financial crises, bankruptcies of listed issuers and credit institutions, and even the violations of the rights of minority shareholders".

Historically, Latvia's market and ownership structure stems almost entirely from the government's establishment of the market in the mid-1990s through the privatisation of state-owned enterprises. The Latvian Privatisation Agency (LPA), created in 1994, focused on identifying strategic investors, which often led to management, employees or other insiders controlling ownership. This was coupled with a second aim to promote widespread share ownership for ordinary citizens through a privatisation certificate scheme. This concentrated control and dispersal of smaller holdings has continued to be the predominant ownership structure of listed companies in Latvia since that time.

Since the founding of the Riga Stock Exchange in 1995, only one private company has issued shares on the Exchange: SAF Tehnika, in its 2004 initial public offer. The number of listed companies initially grew rapidly, rising to a peak of 68 in 1998. However, many of these companies were listed on a "free list" subject to little regulation or trading. With the introduction in 2004 of the Financial Instruments Markets Law, whose share ownership rules included a mandatory share takeover bid threshold at 50%, a number of issuers chose to exit the market.[7] By 2007, following these changes and the merger of the "free list" and the secondary list, the number of issues had declined to 42, decreasing further to 25 today.

Even as the number of listed companies declined, market prices rose substantially during this period in parallel with the rapidly growing Latvian economy, with the Riga index increasing from a level of 100 at the beginning of 2000 to a peak value of 759.44 in September 2007. Following the start of the global financial crisis in late 2007, the index dropped sharply to 204.53 in March 2009, just 27% of its peak value (see Figure 2.1). The index, now composed of 26 issuers, had recovered to a level of 437.99 as of 31 August 2015, while still substantially below its peak levels.

Figure 2.1 **OMX Riga Index Value, January 2000 to August 2015**

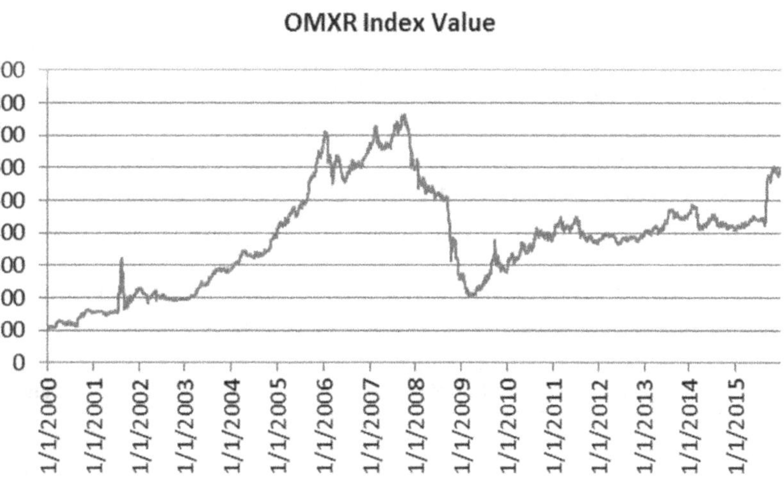

Source: Information provided by Latvian authorities in January 2016.

Meanwhile, the level of market capitalisation and turnover has also declined substantially from 2007 peaks (see Figure 2.2).

Figure 2.2 **Market capitalisation and turnover (EUR millions)**

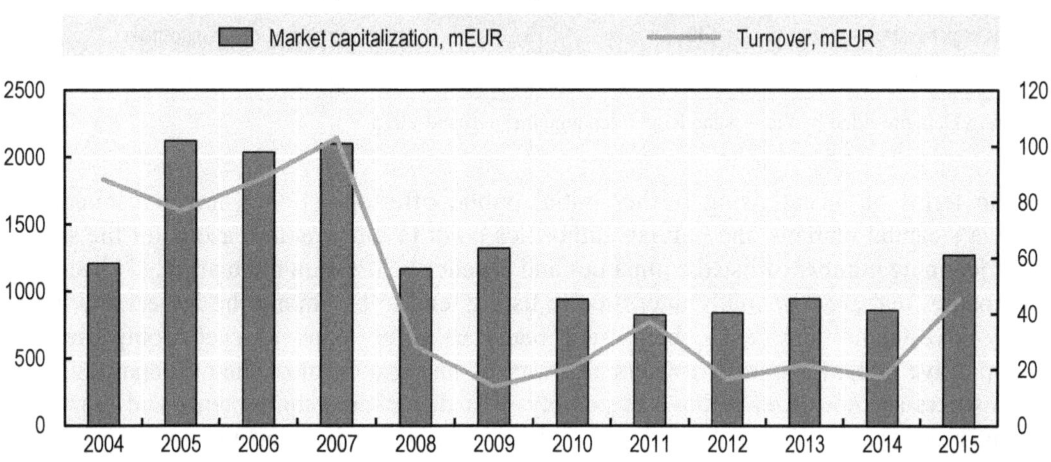

Source: Information provided by Latvian authorities in January 2016.

According to market observers, Latvia's challenges with regard to deepening its capital markets include (1) incentivising more institutional and private investors to engage in the markets and (2) encouraging more companies to raise capital via listing equity and/or debt. (See section 2.1 for more on the Latvian institutional investor profile.)

Regarding the former, Latvian authorities and private sector representatives explain that diversifying Latvia's concentrated corporate ownership remains a significant challenge in terms of both increasing the market's liquidity and addressing the perceived risk of investing in listed Latvian companies. The post-privatisation ownership status quo is perpetuated by the requirement that shareholders, individually or in concert, must issue a mandatory offer to buy out all other shares if they surpass the 50% ownership threshold. As a result, most companies have a single shareholder with just below 50% ownership or several related shareholders who in combination own just below 50% of the shares. Many of the smaller secondary list companies on the market are not actively traded, but the expense of the share buyouts that would be required to delist provides a disincentive to leave the market. The Financial and Capital Market Commission (FCMC) in late 2015 issued a consultation draft proposing amendments to the Financial Instruments Markets Law (FIML, described further in section 2.2) that would lower the buyout threshold to 30% in hopes of facilitating the diversification of corporate ownership among Latvia's listed companies and of securing stronger protections for minority shareholders.

Table 2.3. **Market capitalization of the ten most-traded Latvian companies 1 January – 31 December 2015**

Name	No. of trades	Market cap (EUR)	List/segment	Industry
Olainfarm	2 547	100.1	Baltic Main List	Health care
Ventspils nafta	2 392	476.4	Baltic Main List	Industrials
Grindeks	2 209	49.8	Baltic Main List	Health care
Latvijas kuģniecība	1 917	87.6	Baltic Main List	Industrials
SAF Tehnika	1 449	9.4	Baltic Main List	Technology
Valmieras stikla šķiedra	1 329	81.3	Baltic Secondary List	Basic materials
Latvijas Gāze	1 283	389.4	Baltic Secondary List	Utilities
Latvijas balzams	1 017	45.1	Baltic Secondary List	Consumer goods
Rīgas kuģu būvētava	510	3.3	Baltic Secondary List	Industrials
Ditton pievadķēžu rūpnīca	357	0.6	Baltic Secondary List	Industrials

Source: Data provided by the Nasdaq Riga Exchange through end-2015.

In terms of incentivising further initial public offerings (IPOs) and investment in Latvia's capital markets, the Latvian authorities point to three main reasons for the small and declining number of listed companies and absence of IPOs on the market: (1) because companies that are potentially interested in listing tend to be among the largest and least risky investments for banks, banks are ready to offer loans to such companies at competitive rates; (2) current owners are wary of losing control of their companies; and (3) owners are not eager to have to comply with disclosure requirements and fear that being more transparent could undermine their competitive position vis-a-vis non-listed companies. A fourth reason – one cited by private sector analysts – is the fear that share values may be discounted due to concerns about share liquidity as well as past market scandals (see, for example, Box 2.2 on the Latvian Shipping Company in section 2.2).

The issues of market reputation and the adequacy of the enforcement framework are discussed in greater depth later in this chapter, under section 2.2, which deals with the overall effectiveness of the corporate governance framework.

Considering the perceived riskiness and illiquidity of Latvia's capital market, an alternative incentive for investors to buy shares can be the offering of dividends. However, as Figure 2.3 shows, the number of companies providing dividends has also declined in parallel with the number of listed companies.

Figure 2.3. **Number of listed companies and companies paying dividends**

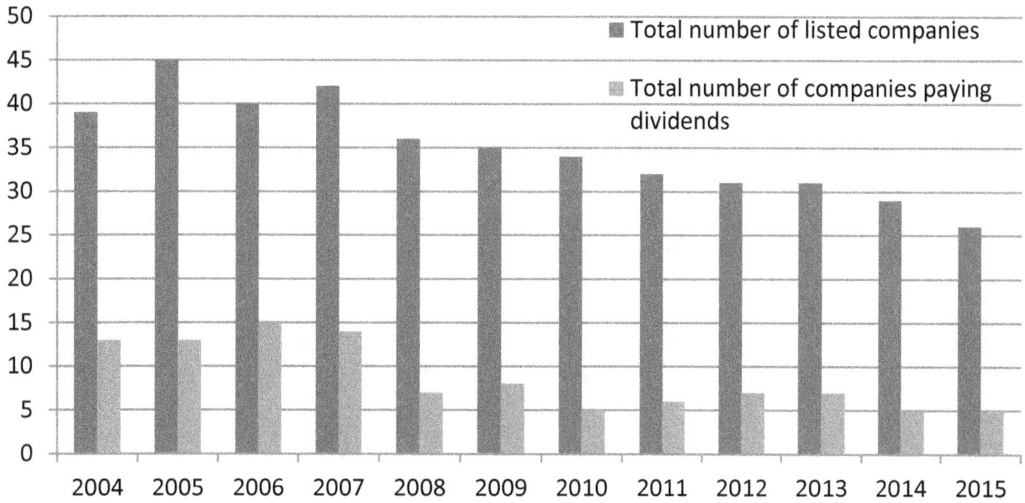

Source: Information provided by Latvian authorities in January 2016.

On the other hand, stock market and government officials are more positive about the relatively greater activity of the corporate bond market as a financing vehicle for Latvian companies. By end-2015, 14 companies – including Latvia's largest company, state-owned Latvenergo – had 42 corporate debt securities listed on the Exchange, with a total nominal value of EUR 950.4 million. There were 12 initial listings by two companies in 2012, another 11 new listings by two companies in 2013, six companies with 13 new listings in 2014, and five companies with 15 listings through 2015, according to Exchange figures. None of these companies has chosen to list shares on the market. In addition to equities and bonds, the exchange also trades government bonds and investment fund securities (see Table 2.4).

Table 2.4. **Securities traded on Nasdaq Riga (as of 31 December 2015)**

Security	Number of Issuers	Capitalization (EUR millions)
Investment funds	5	-
Corporate debt securities	42	932
Government debt securities	12	1165

Source: Nasdaq Riga (www.nasdaqbaltic.com/market/?lang=en) and data provided by Latvian authorities as of January 2016.

The Foreign Investors Council in Latvia (FICIL) has advocated a range of improvements in corporate governance and other measures to spur the development of Latvia's capital markets. A 2011 FICIL position paper asserts that increasing the development of Latvia's capital markets to the level of Estonia's would boost the annual growth rate of Latvia's real GDP per capita by 1.8%, thereby closing the income gap between the two countries by one-third in five years and generating an additional EUR 120 million in tax revenue per year. The report focuses on the importance of improving corporate governance of SOEs and using SOE privatisation to spur capital market development – learning from the experience of other countries such as Poland, which has had success with this model. (FICIL also advocates improvements in enforcement.) Similarly, the April 2015 Nasdaq Baltic study on promoting economic growth in the Baltic region through IPOs also advocates more listing of SOEs, along with other recommendations targeting both potential issuers and investors (see Table 2.5).

Table 2.5. **Nasdaq Baltic recommendations targeting issuers and investors to increase IPOs in Baltic markets**

Recommendations targeting issuers	Recommendations targeting investors
The following measures are recommended to increase the number of potential issuers considering primary offerings and secondary trading on Baltic markets:	*The following measures are meant to facilitate increased investment by institutional and private investors on Baltic markets:*
• **Increase public awareness and perceptions of listing** – for example, by organizing roundtables with the media and positively recognizing issuers (e.g. through market awards). • **Attract private companies** that are suitable for listing – for example, by encouraging private investors to exit from investments through the Exchange and by supporting SME growth, including via listing on the alternative First North Baltic exchange. • Encourage **investor relations and good corporate governance** – for example, by reviewing compliance with corporate governance codes across the Baltic region and by providing guidelines, templates and similar services to facilitate timely and effective disclosures by issuers. • **List shares of SOEs** and encourage SOEs to be more active on the bond market. • **Attract foreign issuers** and encourage Latvian companies listed abroad to **also list at home**. • **Reduce perceived barriers to listing**, including by ensuring local requirements are in line with EU standards (including IFRS and reporting requirements).	• **Expand the local retail investor base** through increased public awareness, access to research and statistics on issuers, and through broadened investment opportunities, among other measures. • **Expand the international retail investor base** by more actively promoting the Baltic market and issuers, providing greater access to issuer information, and better access to trading. • **Attract local and international institutional investors** – for example, by listing and/or increasing the free floats of large, well-performing SOEs; encouraging pension fund managers to invest more at home; and facilitating greater cross-border access among Baltic markets. • **Reform taxation rules and incentives with regard to long-term investment in Baltic markets** – for example, by establishing tax incentives for long-term minor holdings and tax breaks on dividends, and by decreasing the frequency of required tax declarations.

Source: Nasdaq Baltic (2015), Promoting Baltic Economic Growth through IPOs: Study and Action Proposals.

The Latvian government has a list of SOEs and state-owned shares in corporate entities that were recommended for State divestment by a working group appointed by the prime minister to evaluate State ownership in each of Latvia's SOEs. (See also section 3.3 regarding the aforementioned assessment and sections 2.3-4 for an overview of the

SOE sector.) While most recent privatisations involve solicitations of interest from private buyers, joint strategies involving both private buyers and IPOs have also been at least initially considered with respect to the possible privatisations of some of the larger SOEs. To date, however, the government has opted for selling shares to private strategic investors. For example, in Latvia's latest major privatisation, the LPA completed on 20 April 2015 the sale of its 75% stake in Citadele to U.S.-based Ripplewood Advisors LLC and 12 international investors for EUR 74.7 million.[8]

Institutional Investors

Institutional investors do not play a major role in the Latvian equity market. Latvia's self-assessment data indicate that, as of 31 December 2013, 67.82% of share ownership was held by legal persons, another 17.5% by natural persons, and just 10.41% by investment funds. (Custodian banks hold the remaining 4.17%.) Pension funds are the largest single investor group in the Baltics, but their investments in domestic assets are small: the average share of the home market in Latvian pension funds' asset allocation was less than 1% as of mid-2014.

Banks (including foreign branches) dominate the financial markets, accounting for EUR 29.2 billion in assets and 90% of the assets in the Latvian financial system, according to the Latvian authorities. The second largest asset holders are state pension investment plans, whose EUR 1.7 billion in assets account for 5.2%, and insurance funds (including foreign insurance branches) holding EUR 771 million, or 2.4% of the assets in the financial system.

Market analysts and investors (including bank representatives) interviewed for this report stated that there is scepticism about the capital markets, a perception that they are too small, too illiquid, and too risky to invest in. Their reticence is reinforced by the lack of dividends (only 5 of 26 listed companies issued dividends in 2015) and what they assert are low price-to-earnings ratios.

A slight majority of shareholders are Latvian residents (52%), and 48% are non-residents. Germany (17%), Switzerland (9%) and Russia (8%) are the largest non-resident shareholders, followed by Estonia (5%), Lithuania (5%) and Curaçao (2%), according to data provided by the Latvian Central Depository in late 2014.

Latvian authorities also reported combined data covering all emissions of securities (shares, debt securities, and investment fund certificates) registered through the Latvian Central Depository. While natural and legal persons remain the dominant owners (61.35%), investment funds play a much larger role (31.8%) when additional securities instruments are included.

Information on shareholder identities is publicly available via the company profiles on the Nasdaq Riga website for shareholders with at least a 5% ownership stake; in general shares are held either by individuals or corporations. Two listed companies also reported having other financial institutions as significant (but not controlling) shareholders. In a few cases, companies have listed Swedbank AS Clients Accounts as nominee accounts without identifying the ultimate beneficial owner. Companies (and banks as custodians of the shares) are not required to make information on ultimate beneficial owners public, but the regulatory authorities report that they have access to this information for enforcement purposes. Requirements for disclosure of ultimate beneficial owners are described in greater detail under section 3.2.

Although most companies obtain financing through bank loans rather than via capital markets in Latvia, venture capital funds are playing a growing, if still small, role. A 2014 study commissioned by the Ministry of Economics, reviewing small and medium-sized enterprises' (SME) access to finance for the period 2007-13, found that EUR 576 million was made available through a variety of financial instruments.[9] The study concluded that the venture capital market provided 10.7% of this financing (EUR 61.5 million), but that the vast majority of this, EUR 50 million, was publicly funded. It further noted that there were seven venture capital funds active in Latvia in 2014, six of which were publicly funded.[10] A much smaller portion of the financing – 2.1% – came from private equity seed and start-up capital and pre-seed capital that were also almost entirely publicly funded to address what the study referred to as "market failure regarding the undeveloped venture capital market in Latvia." The remaining 87.2% of corporate finance was provided through loans and debt instruments of various categories.

Supervisory Boards

Latvian companies are overseen by a two-tier system of supervisory boards and management boards.[11] Board duties and liability to act in the interests of the company are defined primarily in the CL, as well as in the FIML, and are guided by the Nasdaq Riga's *Rules on Listing and Trading* ("The Nasdaq Listing Rules") and *Principles of Corporate Governance and Recommendations on their Implementation* ("the Nasdaq Principles"). (See also section 2.2.) As per the CL (Art. 292), board responsibilities include: electing and recalling members of the management board; monitoring that the company's business is conducted in accordance with the law, its articles of association, and shareholders' decisions; examining the company's annual accounts and proposals for the use of profits; representing the company in court; supervising related party transactions; reviewing and opining on issues prepared for shareholder meetings; and approving decisions to increase a company's equity capital and to amend the articles of association.[12]

Supervisory boards of commercial enterprises comprise a minimum of three members (for private companies) or five members (for publicly listed companies) and a maximum of 20 members; supervisory board members cannot simultaneously serve on the same company's management board or on that of any dependent company. Shareholders elect directors to terms that cannot exceed five years. There are no specific statutory requirements related to director independence, though the Nasdaq Principles of Corporate Governance recommend independence measures for the supervisory boards of listed companies.[13]

2.2. The Corporate Governance Framework

Latvia is a civil law country. Its legal system – including the Constitution, company law, administrative procedure law, and group-of-companies law – is closely modelled on Germany's. The hierarchy of law consists of the Constitution (*Satversme*), laws, regulations of the Cabinet of Ministers, and binding regulations of local governments. The law of Latvia is divided into private and public law. In general, private law consists of civil law and company law. Public law consists of international law, constitutional law, administrative law, criminal law, financial law and procedural law. The Company Law, Financial Instruments Market Law, the Group of Companies Law, the Nasdaq Listing Rules and the Nasdaq Principles are the main written sources for corporate governance in Latvia.

Legal Framework

Commercial Law

The CL, which came into force on 1 January 2002, governs the establishment, activities and liquidation of companies and partnerships. It prescribes the basic rules for corporate governance – the rights and duties of shareholders, and requirements related to annual general meetings, extraordinary general meetings, supervisory boards and management boards. It also stipulates the information that is to be registered in the Register of Enterprises, which is to be made publicly available either directly from the Register (administered by the Ministry of Justice), as published in the official gazette *Latvijas Vestnesis*, or as delegated to third-party websites such as *www.lursoft.lv*, *www.firmas.lv*, and *www.crediweb.lv*, which charge for access to the information. Latvian authorities state that all relevant European Union directives have been transposed to the CL.[14]

Financial Instruments Market Law

The FIML came into force on 1 January 2004 and replaced the Law on Securities. The purpose of the FIML is to ensure the functioning of the financial instruments market by fostering (1) protection of the interests of investors, (2) the stability and credibility of the financial instruments market, and (3) the availability of information and equal opportunities for all participants in the financial instruments market.

The FIML establishes the procedures by which financial instruments are publicly offered and circulated, the requirements for admission of financial instruments to trading on regulated markets, and requirements for disclosure. The FIML stipulates the information to be provided on a regular basis, including the obligations of a capital company issuing transferable securities to provide information to shareholders relevant to the exercise of their rights. In addition, it includes provisions for the acquisition of major holdings, share buyout offers, the prohibition of the use of inside information, as well as operation of the Latvian Central Depository (LCD) and regulated market organiser (Nasdaq Riga). The FIML includes provisions on investment services and ancillary (non-core) investment services, and the procedures for the licensing and supervision of participants in the financial instruments market. Additionally, it establishes the rights and obligations for participants in the financial instruments market, and prescribes liability for infringing the requirements of the law. The FIML also prescribes the procedures for exchange of information between the competent authorities of the European Union and foreign countries. Latvian authorities report that all relevant European Union directives have been transposed to the FIML.[15] (See also section 2.2 regarding enforcement of the FIML and section 3.1 on FIML provisions prohibiting insider trading and other forms of market abuse.)

At the time of writing, the FCMC and Ministry of Finance had prepared a series of significant amendments to the FIML; these are described in greater detail in section 3.2.

Group of Companies Law

Latvia's Group of Companies Law (GCL) was established to protect creditors and minority shareholders of controlled companies and to establish requirements for their management. It establishes two types of company groups: contractual groups, which are based on written agreements; and factual or *de facto* groups, which exist when a company has controlling influence over another company without formal written agreement.[16]

When contractual agreements are in place, the controlling company has more extensive rights, for example to give instructions to the management board of a controlled company even in cases that may cause damages to the controlled company if they conform to the interests of the group of companies. Although the management board of the controlled company has a duty to implement the instructions issued by the controlling company, the management board of the controlled company still owes its duties only to the controlled company, leaving some legal uncertainty as to how these duties should be resolved when they come into conflict.

Shareholders of companies that are subject to the GCL face requirements mandating them to disclose changes in their ownership, including the beneficial owner of the shares, once they exceed the 10% threshold and for every increase or decrease of 5% occurring above the 10% threshold.

A key provision of the GCL aimed at ensuring minority shareholder rights establishes that contractual company groups with domination or profit transfer agreements have an obligation to determine an appropriate annual compensation for minority shareholders.[17] In addition, where such agreement exists, the controlling company has a duty to acquire shares of a minority shareholder if requested by the minority shareholder.

For factual groups without contractual agreements between the parent and subsidiary companies, a controlled company is obliged to prepare consolidated annual accounts, including a report on relations to the controlling enterprise, known as a report on dependency. The report must be prepared for each accounting year and should state all legal transactions concluded with the controlling company or affiliated companies, that are in the interests of such companies, or that involve a transaction between the controlled company and third persons that is concluded upon the request of the controlled company.

Following a review of consolidated annual account submissions, the Ministry of Justice reported that Latvia has 300 factual groups, including 13 listed companies that are considered to be controlling companies of such groups that may submit consolidated accounts based on IFRS. There are 41 existing contractual groups of companies for which agreements are registered in the Enterprise Register. Among these is one controlling listed company, Daugavpils Lokomotivju Remonta Rupnica, which has entered into 14 domination and profit transfer agreements.[18]

Other Relevant Laws and Regulations

Other relevant laws include (1) the Law on Accounting, which is the main law in the area of accounting in Latvia, and (2) the Annual Accounts Law and the Consolidated Annual Accounts Law, which formerly set forth requirements for financial reporting but were replaced in January 2016 with the entry into force of the new Annual Accounts and Consolidated Annual Accounts Law, adopted by Parliament on 22 October 2015. (The requirements of these laws are described in greater detail with respect to Principles V.B. on accounting and non-financial disclosure standards, and Principle V.C dealing with external audit, in section 3.2). The legal rights of stakeholders are established through the Latvian Constitution and laws including the Consumer Rights Protection Law, Labour Law, Environmental Protection Law, Environmental Impact Assessment Law, and Law on Insolvency (see section 3.5).

Various tax laws are also relevant to the development of Latvia's capital markets. The Law on Enterprise Income Tax requires companies to withhold 10% of dividends provided to resident shareholders. However, since 1 January 2013, no withholding or corporate income tax is applied to corporate resident shareholders. In addition, capital gains are treated as ordinary income for individuals, but since 2013 have been exempt for the purpose of corporate income tax. Finally, Latvian authorities report that legal persons (including SOEs) may be held liable for crimes under Latvia's Criminal Law (Arts. 12 and 70^1).[19]

The Nasdaq Riga Listing Rules and its "comply or explain" Corporate Governance Principles also represent important components of the corporate governance legal framework, and are addressed in greater detail below, assessing the role of stock exchange regulatory requirements in the effectiveness of the corporate governance framework.

Recent changes to the legal framework

The 2014 assessments of Latvia's position relative to the Principles and the SOE Guidelines highlighted a few areas of concern regarding Latvia's legal corporate governance landscape. These include: the effectiveness of the enforcement framework, including the availability of reliable alternative dispute resolution mechanisms (such as arbitration and mediation) to ease pressure on Latvia's post-crisis court system; the insolvency framework; the audit framework; and the legal framework for corporate governance of state-owned enterprises. This section summarizes changes made, as of mid-2016, to the framework in Latvia for alternative dispute resolutions and the framework for audit. The upcoming section dealing with the effectiveness of the corporate governance framework (section 2.2) describes actions and plans with respect to improving enforcement. Recent insolvency reforms are described in section 3.5 (Principle IV.F) dealing with the treatment of stakeholders; and reforms to the SOE corporate governance legal framework are described in section 2.4.

Mediation and Arbitration Laws

Latvia has recently taken steps to increase the efficiency and effectiveness with which commercial cases are handled. These have included efforts to strengthen the quality and increase the usage of alternative dispute resolution (ADR) mechanisms like mediation and arbitration.

The **Law on Mediation** entered into force on 18 June 2014 and governs mediation of civil matters. Its purpose is to facilitate the use of mediation as an ADR and to provide a uniform interpretation of concepts related to the mediation process. It establishes principles and processes for the conduct of mediation, including (1) voluntary participation (2) confidentiality 3) equality and co-operation of parties and (4) neutrality and disinterest of a mediator in the outcome. The Mediation Law and related amendments to the Civil Procedure Law determine the means by which a judge can suggest mediation to resolve a civil dispute.[20] In cases where both parties are willing to consider settling their civil dispute via mediation, they can do so upon recommendation of a court or a judge (Art. 17), who invites the parties to choose a mediator from a list of certified mediators. Latvian authorities estimate that, in 2013, mediation was used in almost 800 cases, 12% of which concerned commercial disputes.

Chapter V of the Mediation Law also includes measures to professionalise the mediator profession by requiring a certification exam and continuing education courses in order to be listed as a certified mediator. These provisions are complemented by the August 2014 Cabinet Resolution No. 433, "Procedure for Certification and Attestation of Mediators". The resolution provides for, among other provisions, procedures for certifying mediators, the content and procedure for certification examinations, as well as the operational procedures and competencies of the Certification and Attestation Commission of Mediators, established under Art. 20 of the Law on Mediation, which include organizing the annual mediator certification examination. Latvian authorities report that the first mediators' certification examination was held in October 2014. At the time of writing, the list of certified mediators includes 24 mediators who passed the examination in October 2014 and received a mediator certificate. A second test is scheduled for October 2015.

The **Law on Arbitration** entered into force on 1 January 2015 and is aimed at building confidence in the use of arbitration through the consolidation of arbitration institutions and new requirements aimed to improve the quality of the arbitration processes. For one, the new law includes more stringent requirements for founding a permanent court of arbitration, though it is still possible to establish an "ad hoc arbitration court" for the resolution of a specific dispute. The Law on Arbitration also includes a number of new provisions to regulate the operations of permanent courts of arbitration, including their facilities, personnel, and public communications and disclosure. Finally, the law also provides tougher criteria for qualifying to become an arbitrator, including the requirement that arbitrators must be lawyers. Permanent courts of arbitration had until 1 June 2015 to submit to the Enterprise Register a confirmation of the court's compliance with statutory requirements for establishing and operating such institutions. As of October 2015, the Enterprise Register had registered 83 permanent courts of arbitration.

Proposed changes to the Financial Instruments Market Law (FIML) and related laws

As of early 2016, a series of amendments had been proposed to the FIML to address areas of concern highlighted in this report and in the 2014 Corporate Governance Committee's review of Latvia's corporate governance framework under the Principles.[21]

First, in relation to the FCMC's enforcement capacity, the amendments would *raise the ceiling for sanctions for violations of FIML rules for disclosure of regulated information*, bringing the law in line with the EU Transparency Directive (Directive 2013/50/EU).[22] The proposed amendments would raise the imposable fines against legal persons to either EUR 10 million, up to 5% of the company's total annual turnover, or up to twice of the amount of the profits gained or losses avoided because of the breach (applying whichever is higher). Natural persons are subject to fines of up to EUR 2 million or up to twice the amount of the profits gained or losses avoided because of the breach. These FIML amendments were adopted by Parliament on 26 May 2016 and entered into force on 29 June 2016.

Second, also in relation to the FCMC's enforcement capacity, the amendments would further strengthen applicable *sanctions or administrative measures for market manipulation and insider trading*, in response to the EU market abuse regulation, which must be implemented by national governments by 3 July 2016.[23] These proposed changes include sanctions against natural persons of up to EUR 5 million and sanctions against legal persons of up to EUR 15 million or 15% of the company's total annual turnover, whichever is higher. These amendments were also adopted by Parliament on 26 May 2016 and entered into force on 29 June 2016.

The Ministry of Justice also proposed parallel amendments to the Criminal Law to implement the Market Abuse Directive, increasing the maximum terms of imprisonment for natural persons to four years for insider dealing and market manipulation for a nonaggravated offence, up to one year of imprisonment for an aggravated offence (if committed by an organised group), and two years for unlawful disclosure of inside information. These changes to the Criminal Law were adopted in January 2016 and entered into force on 1 March 2016. The Ministry of Justice also proposed changes to the Law on the Procedures for the Coming into Force and Application of the Criminal Law that would more clearly define "serious consequences" in financial markets, which could facilitate greater enforcement of the abovementioned provisions. (The prosecution must prove "serious harm" in insider trading and market manipulation cases in order to bring such a case and request the application of sanctions.) The changes to the Law on the Procedures for the Coming into Force and Application of the Criminal Law were adopted by Parliament in January 2016 and entered into force on 1 March 2016. (See also section 3.1)

Third and finally, amendments to the FIML and the Law on Sworn Auditors that were prepared by the Ministry of Finance in early 2016, if enacted and implemented, would address the Corporate Governance Committee's concerns regarding the role, composition, and responsibilities of audit committees of listed companies.[24] The "Amendments to the Law on Sworn Auditors" and "Amendments to the Financial Instruments Market Law" transposing EU Directive 2014/56/EC (the EU amendments to the Audit Directive) – including requirements regarding audit committees – were_adopted during the first of three readings in Parliament on 16 June 2016. The third and final reading was, at the time of writing, expected to take place in early October 2016.

The rules regarding the composition and responsibilities of audit committees that were in force at the time of writing raised two concerns for the Committee in its 2014 review of Latvia's position under the Principles. The first concern relates to the relationship between the supervisory board and the audit committee. Under the FIML in force at the time of writing, there is no requirement for any of the members of the supervisory board to serve on the audit committee. As a result, there is a risk that the supervisory board delegates all financial supervision to the audit committee and is therefore not sufficiently informed to effectively review the company's accounts and internal controls.

In addressing this risk, Latvian authorities indicate that the legislative changes to the FIML and Law on Sworn Auditors introduce the following requirements:

- At least one of the audit committee members must be a member of the supervisory board, in order to ensure higher involvement and accountability of the supervisory board in matters delegated by law to the audit committee.
- The audit committee must report to the supervisory board on its findings.
- The supervisory board is required to include in its written report to the shareholders meeting (as per CL Art. 175) its assessment of the activities of the audit committee, including as an annex the audit committee's annual report.

The second concern that the Committee raised relates to the audit committee's independence from controlling shareholders. Under the current legislative framework, audit committee members are appointed directly by the shareholders and report at least once per year directly to the shareholders. As a result, the controlling shareholder could be in a position to appoint all audit committee members through a majority vote, including even the independent member of the committee.

Regarding this concern, the Latvian authorities state that legislative changes to the FIML would prescribe requirements regarding the election of audit committee members. The draft law would provide that, similar to CL rules for nominating candidates to supervisory boards, all shareholders with at least 5% of voting rights are entitled to nominate their candidates for election of audit committee members. Candidates may be nominated by a shareholder or group of shareholders, but each candidate must have support from not less than 5% of the capital with voting rights represented at the annual general meeting (AGM). All shareholders then vote for their preferred candidates via a ballot vote, and a shareholder may vote for one or more candidates. Independent members of the audit committee would also be required to confirm in writing that they meet the law's independence requirements.

Institutional framework

The Ministry of Justice and Ministry of Finance both have responsibilities with respect to the legal framework for corporate governance. The Ministry of Justice maintains the national register of companies and has responsibility for developing amendments to the CL and GCL. The Ministry of Justice also has responsibilities with respect to the Law on Insolvency and the functioning of the courts.[25] The Ministry of Finance takes the lead role with respect to the FIML and oversight of accounting and auditing laws, as well as the accounting and audit professions. Since June 2015, the Cross-Sectoral Coordination Centre takes the lead with respect to laws dealing with state-owned enterprises (see section 2.4).

The Financial and Capital Market Commission (FCMC) is responsible for enforcing the FIML, among its overall responsibility to supervise banks, insurance, and the securities market. It also oversees private pension funds, investment funds and their managers, payment institutions and electronic money institutions. In executing its responsibilities, the FCMC co-operates with the Bank of Latvia, Ministry of Finance, Justice, Financial Intelligence Unit, Consumer Rights Protection Centre, Cabinet of Ministers and Parliament.

The securities market is managed by Nasdaq Riga, which, along with Nasdaq stock exchanges in Tallinn and Vilnius, make up the Nasdaq Baltic Securities Market. Nasdaq Riga also owns the LCD, which is the national depository responsible for custody and settlement of all publicly issued and circulated securities issued in Latvia. Nasdaq is responsible for enforcing its listing requirements and the Nasdaq Principles of Corporate Governance and, in so doing, cooperates regularly with the FCMC. Its role is described in greater detail under "Principle I.D" in the next section, which deals with the overall effectiveness of the corporate governance framework.

Overall effectiveness of the corporate governance framework

This section assesses Latvia's corporate governance framework against key recommendations in Chapter 1 of the Principles. It therefore builds on the previous introduction of Latvia's corporate governance framework and assesses its implementation in practice, according to Principles 1.A to 1.F. Taken together, the discussion of Latvia's corporate governance framework for listed companies is distinct from – but linked to – Latvia's corporate governance framework for state-owned enterprises, described following this section (section 2.4).

Corporate governance framework (Principle 1.A)

The over-arching recommendation in Chapter 1 of the Principles is that "The corporate governance framework should promote transparent and fair markets, and the efficient allocation of resources. It should be consistent with the rule of law and support effective supervision and enforcement." **Principle 1.A** further specifies that the corporate governance framework should be developed with a view to its impact on overall economic performance, market integrity and the incentives it creates for market participants and the promotion of transparent and well-functioning markets.

Latvian authorities, in their self-evaluation under the Principles submitted to the Secretariat for the purposes of this review, consider this recommendation fully implemented, asserting that both the FIML and CL are designed to promote economic efficiency and market integrity by setting regulations that sustain economic growth and incorporate the best practices from internal and international experiences (including the requirements of the EU legislation). These are complemented by Nasdaq OMX listing rules applying to listed companies and voluntary, comply-or-explain recommendations on corporate governance contained in the Nasdaq Principles, which provide high levels of transparency regarding corporate governance practices among listed companies in the market.

All main amendments to these laws are adopted only after consultation with the public and private sectors, including representatives of non-governmental organisations and investors. The Council of State Secretaries decides when laws are submitted to the public for consultation via public announcements on the government's website, subject to a 2.5-week public consultation period. When drafting amendments, the legislator must consider the likely costs and benefits of the proposed changes. The institution responsible for drafting amendments to the existing laws or regulations or drafting a new law has a duty to prepare an impact assessment (or "annotation") for the proposed amendment or law, and to collect and address public comments. Outside of this process, the government reports that it is in regular consultation with stakeholders and generally establishes a working group to provide input to significant legislation.

European Union directives have been a major influence on the legal framework for corporate governance of listed companies. While some companies have "pushed back" on disclosure requirements as too burdensome and such requirements have been cited as a disincentive for some companies to list, the FCMC suggested that the directives do not provide much flexibility to relax such requirements. It is also worth noting that the more-relaxed disclosure requirements of the Nasdaq Baltic First North alternative, non-regulated listing segment have not been successful in attracting new Latvian companies to the market.[26]

Consistency with the rule of law, transparency, and enforcement (Principle 1.B)

Principle I.B states that the legal and regulatory requirements that affect corporate governance practices in a jurisdiction should be consistent with the rule of law, transparent and enforceable.

The Latvian self-evaluation states that it fully implements this recommendation, ensuring that legal requirements are transparently enacted and reasonably foreseeable – by, for example, providing a sufficient and reasonable transition period for new legal requirements. The legal framework provides a complementary set of laws governing corporate governance practices, including the Company Law, the Financial Instruments

Market Law, the Nasdaq listing requirements and other laws previously cited in the landscape section of this report.

Public enforcement of the corporate governance framework

How effectively the laws and regulations of the corporate governance framework are enforced is a key question for this review. The self-evaluation states that the rules are enforced mainly by bringing a civil action against the infringing party or by dismissing the management or supervisory board member. However, in accordance with the FIML, the Law on the Financial and Capital Market Commission and other laws, public enforcement of the corporate governance rules is also possible. The FCMC is entitled to ensure the functioning of the financial instruments market (for instance, the FCMC controls conformity with the laws, regulations and decisions that it has adopted) and to govern activities of financial and capital market participants, as well as to apply sanctions (fines, suspension of the trade of securities, etc.) if the rules are infringed. Secondly, if infringement of the rules of corporate governance includes fraud or other illegal actions, criminal liability may be imposed on the infringer. Thus, the rules of corporate governance are enforced either by private or public enforcement, and infringement of the rules of corporate governance may result in civil, administrative or criminal liability. (Criminal offences are investigated by the Latvian State Police's economic crimes unit, which cooperates to a limited extent with the FCMC.)

Data provided by the FCMC on its enforcement actions from 2009 to 2015 (see Box 2.1) show that most activity has focused on the timeliness of disclosure requirements. Nasdaq has also taken relatively frequent actions to suspend trading, particularly in cases when information has been selectively disclosed without disclosure to all market participants. The Latvian Association of Sworn Auditors (LASA), which also plays a role in peer reviewing audits and ensuring compliance with requirements for external auditors and audit firms (with public oversight from the Ministry of Finance), reported issuing 12 suspensions of auditor certificates, 17 warnings and 15 "remarks" since 2010. (See also section 3.2) This system is currently being changed to increase the capacity and independence of mechanisms to supervise the audit profession by designating a competent authority to implement and comply with the new EU Audit Directive and EU Audit Regulation. The directive must be implemented and the new audit regulation must be applicable by mid-2016.

As the main public enforcement body monitoring Latvia's financial securities markets, it should be noted that the FCMC's actions have mostly involved corrective measures or warnings rather than fines, and that the highest fine levied by FCMC in the last six years has been only EUR 8 500. The FCMC was much more active in applying 34 corrective measures during the same period, also mostly related to disclosure. Although the FCMC data did not report individually on the reasons for the corrective measures, it reported that corrective measures are generally applied if the violation is inessential (for example, disclosure is delayed by only a few days, or the inaccuracies are minor), and the issuer has not committed any previous breaches. Only three FCMC fines issued during this period were unrelated to disclosure – a 2010 fine for failure to establish an audit committee in a timely manner, and two 2009 fines for failure to make mandatory share buy-out offers after a shareholder exceeded the 50% ownership threshold (the shareholders subsequently decreased their holdings below 50% to avoid having to make mandatory offers).

Box 2.1. **FCMC enforcement statistics under the FIML, 2009-15**

2015	• In one administrative case, the FCMC imposed a fine on an issuer of EUR 5 000. The fine was applied because the publication of the issuer's financial statements was delayed. • In one case, the FCMC issued a warning because an issue delayed publication of its financial statements. • In six cases, the FCMC applied corrective measures regarding financial statements. • In three cases, the FCMC applied corrective measures regarding notification of major holding and in two cases corrective measures regarding notification by the holder of inside information. • In one case, the FCMC applied corrective measures regarding the delay of publication of a significant event. • In one case, the FCMC applied corrective measures regarding equal treatment of all owners of transferable securities that are of one and the same type and class.
2014	• In one administrative case, the FCMC imposed a fine on two persons of EUR 14 200 each. In another case, the FCMC imposed a fine on two persons of EUR 14 200 and EUR 10 650, respectively. The fines were applied to shareholders who obtained a holding of more than 50% of shares without making a mandatory share buy-back offer. The shareholders appealed the FCMC's decisions in both cases. • There were six administrative cases regarding disclosure of regulated information. In two cases, the FCMC issued a warning; in two cases the FCMC imposed a fine of EUR 3 550 and EUR 4 000; in one case the FCMC concluded that the issuer's financial statements did not comply with FIML requirements; and in one case the FCMC decided to remove an issuers' financial instruments from trading. • In five administrative cases involving the notification by the holder of inside information about transactions in an issuer's shares, the FCMC issued a warning in four cases and imposed a fine of EUR 500 in one. • In eight cases, the FCMC applied corrective measures.
2013	• In seven cases the FCMC applied corrective measures to eliminate weaknesses in disclosure of mandatory information. • Two formal warnings were issued to issuers who did not submit financial reports in time. Neither issuer appealed the FCMC's decision.
2012	• In five cases the FCMC applied corrective measures. • In one case the FCMC imposed a fine on issuer of LVL 5 000 (EUR 7 100). The fine was imposed to an issuer who did not timely disclose information on a significant agreement. The issuer appealed the FCMC's decision. The court of first instance upheld the decision of the FCMC but the issuer appealed again in the next instance. Legal proceeding is ongoing. • In one case the FCMC gave a formal warning to an issuer who did not submit financial reports in time. The issuer did not appeal.

Box 2.1. **FCMC enforcement statistics under the FIML, 2009-15** (cont.)

2011	• In eight cases the FCMC applied corrective measures. • In three cases the FCMC imposed fines on issuers of LVL 1 000 (EUR 1 400), LVL 2 500 (EUR 3 500) and LVL 3 000 (EUR 4 200). In all three cases issuers did not submit financial reports in time. Issuers did not appeal.
2010	• In nine cases the FCMC applied corrective measures. • Three formal warnings were issued to issuers. In two cases issuers did not submit financial reports in time and in one case issuer did not timely disclose information on a significant event. Issuers did not appeal. • In one case the FCMC imposed a fine of LVL 5 000 (EUR 7 100) on an issuer who did not submit financial report in time for the second year in a row. In addition, the FCMC ordered an issuer to publish financial report in certain period of time. The issuer appealed, but the court upheld the FCMC's decision. • In one case a penalty of LVL 5 000 (EUR 7 100) was imposed on an issuer for non-compliance with FIML requirements relating to the establishment of an audit committee. The issuer did not appeal.
2009	• In five cases the FCMC applied corrective measures. • In one case the FCMC imposed a fine on an issuer of LVL 1 000 (EUR 1 400) and in three cases the FCMC issued formal warnings; in all four cases issuers had not submitted financial reports in time. Issuers did not appeal. • In addition, the FCMC separately reported that two fines of LVL 6 000 (EUR 8 500) and LVL 5 000 (EUR 7 100) were applied to shareholders who obtained a holding of more than 50% of shares without making a mandatory share buy-back offer. The shareholders appealed in both cases and subsequently reduced their holdings to comply with the law, but the court upheld both decisions.

Source: Information provided by Latvian authorities through February 2016.

FCMC reported also investigating an average of up to 20 cases a year of potential insider trading and market manipulation, and referring one to two cases per year to the police for possible criminal prosecution. However, there have not been any successful criminal prosecutions of insider trading cases, and market participants interviewed for this report suggested that economic crimes in general are not given high priority.

As described above, to implement the EU regulation on market abuse and the EU Transparency Directive, the Ministry of Justice and FCMC have proposed amendments to the FIML and CL that would provide for stronger sanctions (prison and fines) against natural and legal persons for criminal cases of market abuse, as well as higher fines for administrative sanctions. (See section 2.2) According to the FCMC, the ability to prosecute administrative cases involving the use of privileged information or market manipulation would be welcome as it would increase the FCMC's flexibility to intervene more directly in such cases. Strengthened sanctioning capabilities are complemented by a closer programme of co-operation between police, prosecutors and the FCMC, which will include joint seminars dealing with enforcement issues and greater use of FCMC staff to advise police and prosecutors on securities market–related cases.

Private enforcement and Latvia's court system

The relatively low number of significant cases, low fines and narrow scope of public enforcement activities to date and the fact that the Latvian authorities characterise enforcement as mainly handled through private actions under civil law point to the functioning of the Latvian court system as a key factor in the effectiveness of enforcement.

The Committee's 2014 assessment of Latvia's corporate governance framework highlighted concerns, expressed by international observers and the private sector, over the efficiency of Latvian courts. Criticisms of the length of time needed to resolve cases, backlog, and abuses of the system have been raised, particularly in the context of Latvia's large volume of insolvency cases following the financial crisis.[27]

The FICIL has issued position papers on capital markets development (FICIL, 2011) and on facilitating efficiency of the court system that both call for measures to enhance the efficiency of the judicial system, including the following:

- Establishing specialisation of judges on financial markets rules and regulations, as well as international market practice by providing training and technical assistance;
- Establishing separate courts to hear commercial and capital markets disputes, which would also provide for an effective fast track procedure;
- Improving enforcement of foreign court rulings and foreign law, as well as the normative regulation of immediate enforcement of a court judgement.

The Latvian government has taken numerous steps to address the above concerns. One reform, launched in May 2013, was to increase the number of cases contesting decisions by the AGM/EGM heard by the Jelgava City Court, which has exclusive competence to examine these types of disputes. In accordance with the Civil Procedure Law, the new special civil procedure handled through Jelgava City Court applies to claims for contesting decisions by the AGM/EGM concerning amendments to the articles of association, increases or reductions of equity capital, termination of activities of a company, reorganisation of a company, entering into a group of companies' agreement, amending or termination thereof. The court examines claims by written procedure if the parties do not request examination of the matter in court or the court does not consider a physical hearing necessary. The parties, as well as judges, have definite time limits for several legal proceedings. A court judgment may be appealed at the appellate level, but only in accordance with cassation procedures established at the Supreme Court level.[28] Thus, court examinations concerning such claims are faster than the ordinary ones. As of July 2014, 39 cases had been decided, each generally taking just 20-40 days to resolve.

Other reforms have dealt with clarifying the roles of first-level courts, appeals courts and the court of cassation (i.e. the Supreme Court). The civil procedure was also amended to increase judicial capacity by allowing judges to (1) decide cases in absentia (since parties had been forcing delays in cases by not showing up), (2) discipline parties that fail to submit evidence in due time, (3) increase the efficiency of court communications with parties, and (4) carry out other changes to increase the effectiveness of civil procedures. In addition, amendments to the Civil Procedure Law were adopted in 2014 and 2015 to introduce the possibility to redistribute case files (i.e. transferring the case to another court) if the case is not heard on its own merits and if the transfer of the case can achieve a quicker trial. Another important step to increase judicial capacity was taken by assigning 10 extra judges to Riga city courts, where backlogs have been highest. The Judicial Council and the cabinet ministers have also aimed to consolidate the administration of individual courts within certain geographic regions in order to find further efficiencies. The Ministry of Justice reported that cases outside Riga generally are resolved in 3-6 months, whereas Riga cases can take up to a year to resolve. The 10 extra judges should increase capacity by about 5%, according to the Ministry.

In addition, a technical assistance programme to implement the use of videoconferencing, sound recording and other information technologies to improve the efficiency of court proceedings was implemented beginning in 2013, along with the establishment of a professional evaluation programme for judges. Training programmes for judges will also be launched next year as part of a five-year EU-funded initiative to consolidate human resource capacities and develop competencies of judicial and law enforcement staff. The training programme is expected to be launched in the second half of 2016.

Finally, as noted above (section 2.2), Latvia has taken steps to increase the usage of ADR mechanisms like mediation and arbitration, with the entry into force of the new Mediation Law (in June 2014) and the new Arbitration Law (in January 2015). Regarding arbitration, government authorities and private sector representatives alike note that the consolidation and registration of Latvia's arbitration institutions has the potential to positively impact the perception of arbitration as a viable venue for commercial dispute resolution. (The number of permanent arbitration institutions has decreased from 214 at the beginning of 2014 to 83 as of October 2015.)

There is some evidence that the range of efforts is bearing some fruit in terms of a declining backlog of cases, declining length of time of court proceedings at the first-instance level, and a positive clearance rate (more cases being decided than being submitted) since 2012, according to Ministry of Justice data. The *EU 2015 Justice Scoreboard* comparison of average court case times across a range of categories also showed some improvements in Latvia between 2010 and 2013 – particularly in the resolution of administrative cases, where Latvia ranks first in the EU. The time required to resolve insolvency cases in Latvia fell by half, from an average of 3 years in 2010 to 1.5 years in June 2014, placing Latvia 11th among 28 EU countries.[29] The time needed to resolve litigious civil and commercial cases at the first-instance level dropped from an average of 330 days in 2010 to about 250 days in 2012, according to the report, placing Latvia 12th out of 21 countries reporting data. The Ministry of Justice asserts that the issue of backlogs in the courts has now largely been addressed at lower instance levels, although some delays remain at the Supreme Court level that are more difficult to address. These broader trends and the overall effectiveness of the reforms were reviewed by the OECD's Public Governance Committee, and its conclusions have been taken into account.[30]

While taking into account the overall efficiency of the judicial system and the Latvian government's recent reforms, the Committee's review must also focus more specifically on the reliability and effectiveness of the enforcement system with respect to corporate governance of listed companies. In this regard the record appears to show that there has been both active public and private enforcement of corporate governance–related requirements, but that the low level of fines, lack of cases of criminal prosecution and in some cases lengthy court proceedings may hinder the full effectiveness of the enforcement framework.

Box 2.2. **Latvian Shipping Company and Ventspils Nafta**

A dispute involving shareholders of two main-list companies, the Latvian Shipping Company (LSC, or *Latvijas kugnieciba* in Latvian) and Ventspils Nafta (VN), serves to illustrate the type of corporate governance scandal that has damaged confidence in Latvia's capital markets. LSC is a former SOE that has been listed on the main list of the Nasdaq Riga Exchange since 2002. LSC is 49.94% owned by VN, which a second main-list, transit-oriented holding company. The two companies are the largest on the main list of the Riga Exchange, with EUR 112 million and EUR 149 million in market capitalization, respectively, as of the end of 2013, and publish consolidated accounts involving both companies.

The two companies have received particular attention because of high-profile disputes between management and shareholders and media reports of the alleged influence over the two companies (since VN's first stage of privatisation) of Aivars Lembergs, mayor since 1988 of the Latvian port city of Ventspils (and a candidate for prime minister in 2006). According to these reports, Lembergs gained his influence over VN through a company he allegedly partially controlled at that time, "Latvijas Nafta Tranzitz" (LNT),[31] which was VN's largest shareholder (42%) during this first phase of privatisation, while 38.6% was retained by the Latvian government as of 2005. However, in the second stage of VN privatisation in 2006, 34.75% of shareholdings in VN were obtained by Euromin Holdings Limited (indirectly held by the Dutch-founded, Swiss based Vitol shipping group), thereby also making Vitol an indirect shareholder in LSC. By the first half of 2010, Euromin Holdings had increased its shareholdings in VN to 49.5, while LNT remained the second major shareholder of VN, with 43.25% of shares as of 9 October 2013. Major disputes emerged in 2009 and 2010, during which time Vitol representatives took over management of VN (in 2009) and of LSC (in 2010).[32]

Following Vitol's replacement of VN management in 2009, Vitol announced that it had initiated a request for an EGM of LSC shareholders to consider changes to the LSC management and supervisory boards beginning in January 2010. A meeting scheduled on 8 October 2010 was postponed to 17 December, with media reports suggesting that the company's management had used all possible measures to avoid having the EGM – and with LSC even building a fence around its building in the centre of Riga, alleging that a group of shareholders was planning an attack on the building. Although the meeting of 17 December was due to take place at a conference centre in the region of Kuldigas, more than 100 kilometres from Riga, on 16 December LSC announced the meeting would again be postponed, this time to 28 January 2011, due to an electric power outage.[33] However, subsequent reports indicated that shareholders who attempted to go ahead with the EGM on 17 December but were prevented from entering the conference centre by armed guards, persisted in going ahead with the EGM, holding the meeting nearby in a van with eight seats.[34]

With 78.2% of shareholders registered as present, the LSC EGM decided to change the members of both the LSC supervisory board and management board, and to pursue a claim against the previous members of the LSC management board. Although some protests were registered regarding the legitimacy of the decisions taken at the EGM, the Enterprise Register subsequently confirmed the changes to the supervisory and management board.

Competing claims were entered in Riga's courts. Shareholders' claims against one supervisory board member were subsequently enforced through an October 2011 Riga Regional Court decision seizing the property of supervisory board members and awarding LVL 2.56 million (EUR 4 million). The Regional Court's ruling was immediately enforceable and reportedly not subject to appeal.[35] In 2013, the Riga Regional Court ruled against compensation of LVL 10 million sought by LSC. In October 2013, the court revoked its decision on remuneration received by previous management and supervisory board members.

Box 2.2. **Latvian Shipping Company and Ventspils Nafta** (cont.)

Amid all this, the FCMC, during the 2009-10 period of shareholder disputes, had identified violations by both VN and LSC for failures to publish their annual audited reports for 2009 on time. LSC received a warning as a first-time offender, while VN was fined LVL 5 000 (EUR 7 100) because it had already been late in publishing its annual audited report the previous year. A similar violation in relation to LSC's 2010 audit report led to an LVL 3 000 (EUR 4 269) fine. Trading of LSC shares were also suspended for a short period in November 2010 due to insufficient disclosure to the market.

Starting in 2011, LSC made a concerted effort to improve the company's transparency and corporate governance. By 2012 the company had received the Nasdaq Baltic Market award for "Most Visible Improvement in Investor Relations," with a 21.67% improvement in its score. VN came in second place with a 17.95% increase in its score. Among the 13 listed companies monitored by Nasdaq Riga for compliance with the Nasdaq Principles corporate governance recommendations, VN recorded the highest compliance score of any Latvian company (90%), with LSC finishing with the fourth highest score (80%). LSC reported that its corporate governance score had improved by 34% over the level recorded in 2011. In addition, LSC's large losses in 2009-10 also began turning around in 2011, with a 70% decrease in losses reported during the first quarter of 2011, and a return to profits reported for the first time beginning in the first quarter of 2014. On 17 September 2015, Euromin Holdings acquired LNT's entire shareholding in VN, raising its ownership stake in VN to 93.24% and thereby increasing its indirect ownership in LSC. (VN remained LSC's largest shareholder with 49.94% of shares as of September 2015.)

Sources: LSC and VN annual reports, Latvian government, Nasdaq Riga corporate governance scores and website, SSIA website and various press reports.

Data and summaries of court decisions provided by the Ministry of Justice show that there has been substantial court activity on the issue of board member liability. Since 2010 there have been more than 550 decisions at the first-instance level (on board member liability and the right of companies and shareholders to bring actions against their board members), nearly 400 decisions at the appellate level, and 39 cases resolved at the cassation court level. No breakdowns were available on how many of these cases may have affected listed companies, how many decisions held board members liable for damages to the company or the amounts of damages awarded. However, summaries of some of the key decisions did indicate that the courts have established precedents to uphold company and shareholder claims to recover damages to the company due to board members' failure to act in the company's interest (generally involving members of the management board). A smaller number of cases have involved actions by shareholders and board members seeking to void decisions of shareholder meetings under Articles 286 and 287 of the Company Law (featuring 67 court decisions since 2010). Again, more-specific data on the outcomes of these cases and the extent to which they applied to listed companies were not available.

Market analysts and other market participants suggested that a series of highly publicised corporate governance scandals and shareholder disputes involving major Latvian companies such as Liepajas Metalurgs and Ventspils Nafta have hurt the market's reputation, and may have contributed to investors' reluctance to invest in Latvian equity markets. These cases are described in greater detail later in Box 3.4 (see section 3.1) and in Box 2.2. The LSC and Ventspils Nafta case demonstrates the capacity of public enforcement authorities to apply administrative sanctions with relatively low levels of fines. It also shows that more-significant efforts by shareholders to recover damages, and by criminal prosecutors to prosecute economic crimes, have proven to be complex, with frequent delays and sometimes conflicting rulings that have made it difficult to reach clear conclusions. Finally, the LSC/Ventspils Nafta case, in particular, reveals significant recent corporate governance improvements which parallel what appears to be a growing recognition among Latvian listed companies of the importance of corporate governance.

Division of enforcement responsibilities (Principle 1.C)

Principle I.C states that the division of the responsibilities among different authorities should be clearly articulated and designed to serve the public interest.

Latvia's self-evaluation emphasises that the FCMC has the full rights of an independent (autonomous) public institution in its regulation and monitoring of the functioning of the financial and capital market and its participants. The FCMC carries out the supervision of Latvian banks, credit unions, insurance companies and insurance brokerage companies, and participants of the financial instruments market – as well as private pension funds, investment funds and their managers, payment institutions and electronic money institutions. Thus, there is a single, main authority responsible for the financial and capital market.

In addition, the government of Latvia (in particular, the Ministry of Justice, the Ministry of Economics and the Ministry of Finance, in co-operation with the FCMC) is the authority that drafts and approves amendments to the CL, the FIML, tax laws and other laws related to general rules of corporate governance before submitting them to the *Saeima* (the Parliament) for final adoption. The competencies of these institutions are laid down in the laws and by-laws of each institution. There is a clear division of responsibility between these institutions, and their competencies do not appear to overlap.

Earlier in Chapter III we described the different institutions' responsibilities for various elements of the corporate governance and enforcement framework. These included the Ministry of Justice for oversight of the Enterprise Register and development of amendments to insolvency and company laws and the Group of Companies law; the Ministry of Finance for accounting and auditing laws and, as delegated, the LASA for oversight of the audit profession; and the Nasdaq Riga Surveillance Committee for enforcement of listing rules and the monitoring of trading, including actions to suspend trading or place companies on observation status.

Stock market regulation (Principle 1.D)

Principle I.D. states that stock market regulation should support effective corporate governance.

The Nasdaq Listing Rules applying to listed companies and the voluntary, comply-or-explain recommendations on corporate governance contained in the Nasdaq Principles, appear to provide high levels of transparency regarding corporate governance practices among listed companies in the market. Both the FCMC and Nasdaq report strong co-operation on enforcement matters.

As mentioned in section 2.1, the Nasdaq Listing Rules stipulate the requirements for listing and trading of financial instruments, their delisting, requirements for the issuers of these instruments, and the procedures by which the Exchange shall carry out the surveillance of issuers. The size and free float requirements to be eligible for listing on the main list were summarized earlier in section 2, which describe the business environment and capital markets. An additional requirement stipulates that an issuer must have been active in its main field of economic activity for at least three years. There are no quantitative restrictions that apply to issuers on the secondary list. The listing rules, which mainly focus on disclosure, generally correspond to FIML requirements.

The Exchange's principal tool for promoting corporate governance of listed companies is its *Principles of Corporate Governance and Recommendations on their Implementation*, also mentioned earlier in section 2.1. All 26 listed companies on the main and secondary lists are required to disclose either their compliance with the Principles' recommendations, or to explain why a particular recommendation is not being applied.[36] The Principles include 14 main recommendations and 83 sub-recommendations that may be divided into five categories: (1) the organisation of the AGM and EGM; (2) functions and activities of the management board and supervisory board; (3) disclosure and relations of a company with its investors and third parties; (4) internal control and risk management; and (5) remuneration. The specific recommendations and attendant compliance levels are covered in greater detail, as relevant to Latvian implementation of the OECD Principles' recommendations, in Chapter III of this report.

The Nasdaq Principles were first issued by the Exchange in December 2005. Initially, beginning in 2007, only companies on the main list were required to issue reports. The Principles were updated in both 2008 and 2010 to take into account the latest recommendations of the European Commission and, beginning in 2009, all main and secondary list companies were required to submit "comply or explain" reports. All of the reports are published on the website www.oricgs.lv (the Central Storage of Regulated Information, or ORICGS) and also on the Nasdaq Baltic website, and most listed companies also publish them on their own websites. As of 2015, the Stock Exchange actively monitors the report quality of only the five main-list companies and eight secondary-list companies whose market capitalization is above EUR 10 million. Within this group, Ventspils Nafta reported the highest compliance rate of 90% in 2013, but there was substantial variation across monitored companies, with an average of 66% compliance overall (see Table 2.6).

The Exchange's management board, which is responsible for monitoring compliance with the Nasdaq Principles, noted that overall disclosure of companies' compliance has increased in recent years as a result of awareness-raising in the region by the Nasdaq Baltic exchanges. These awareness-raising efforts include the annual Nasdaq Baltic Market Awards, which identify the best companies in the Baltic market in terms of investor relations.[37] Nasdaq Riga reports that the overall compliance with the Nasdaq Principles' investor relations recommendations has improved 21% since the first Baltic Market Awards in 2006. Other private sector representatives during the fact-finding visit also credited the establishment of the Baltic Institute for Corporate Governance (BICG) for raising awareness of the need for corporate governance in Baltic countries' private sectors.

Table 2.6. **Company compliance rates with the Nasdaq Principles of Corporate Governance as of 2013**

Ticker	Company	Compliance level (%)
GRD1R	Grindeks (health care)	81
SAF1R	SAF Tehnika (equipment)	84
VNF1R	Ventspils nafta (industrial services)	90
OLF1R	Olainfarm (health care)	79
LSC1R	Latvijas kuģniecība (Latvian shipping)	80
GZE1R	Latvijas Gāze (Latvian gas)	78
BAL1R	Latvijas balzāms (food & beverage)	49
VSS1R	Valmieras stikla šķiedra (Valmiera fiberglass)	64
DPK1R	Ditton pievadkēžu rupnīca (factory)	57
LJM1R	Latvijas Jūras medicīnas centrs (health care)	63
LME1R	Liepājas metalurgs (metalworks)	47
RKB1R	Rīgas kuģu būvētava (Riga shipyard)	46
LOK1R	Daugavpils Lokomotīvju Remonta rupnīca (locomotive repair)	40
	Average	**66**

Source: Data provided by the Nasdaq Riga Exchange through end-2015.

Integrity and resources of enforcement authorities (Principle 1.E)

Principle I.E states that supervisory, regulatory and enforcement authorities should have the authority, integrity and resources to fulfil their duties in a professional and objective manner. Moreover, their rulings should be timely, transparent, and fully explained.

The Latvian self-evaluation reports that the Law on the Financial and Capital Market Commission provides the FCMC with appropriate authority, rights and resources to fulfil its duties. For instance, the FCMC may issue regulations and take decisions governing the activities of participants in the financial and capital market, request and receive information necessary for execution of its functions, and stipulate restrictions on participants' market activities. Its governance structure and capacity to act independently, in terms of both budget resources and decision-making, were noted earlier in section 2.2. Its decisions are communicated by public announcements, and when the FCMC issues an administrative act (resolution), this resolution may be challenged in the court in accordance with the rules of administrative proceedings.

The Ministry of Finance's current public oversight of LASA, which handles the certification of auditors and ensures the quality of audits, already provides checks and balances that help ensure the integrity of the audit profession. The Ministry of Finance's role is expected be further strengthened as Latvia moves to implement the EU Audit Directive through amendments to the Law on Audit. FCMC's oversight and responsibility for enforcing the FIML help to ensure the Nasdaq Riga's complementary enforcement of listing rules, including those related to trading and disclosure.

Cross-border cooperation (Principle 1.F)

Principle I.F states that cross-border co-operation should be enhanced, including through bilateral and multilateral arrangements for exchange of information.

In Latvia's self-evaluation against the Principles, the FCMC reported that it has not been involved in any cross-border enforcement cases, but that it is a signatory to the International Organization of Securities Regulators (IOSCO) Multilateral Memorandum of Understanding Concerning Consultation and Co-operation and the Exchange of Information.[38] The FCMC indicated that it regularly shares information with other signatories to the IOSCO MMOU, both within and outside of the EU.

2.3. Overview of the SOE Sector

This section provides an overview of Latvia's sector for state-owned enterprises, including the sector's size and composition. Section 2.4, will summarize the legal and regulatory framework for SOE corporate governance, which is further assessed in Chapter IV of this report.

As of September 2015, Latvia's central government fully owned 67 SOEs, owned more than 50% shares in another five enterprises, and owned between 10% and 50% shares in 11 enterprises. The government reported that it holds a minority (less than 10%) share in a further 32 commercial enterprises.[39] Moreover, Latvian SOEs hold shares in 114 other enterprises, with ownership ranging from 0.01% to wholly owned subsidiaries. These figures may change, as Latvian authorities indicate that in 2016 the State will decide on its ownership stake in all SOEs and on their legal status (i.e. possibly transforming some SOEs into public agencies or institutions).[40] Latvian SOEs generally take one of two legal forms: a state-owned joint stock company (JSC, or *akciju sabiedrība*) or a limited liability company (LLC, or *sabiedrība ar ierobežotu atbildību*). There is one statutory corporation, Altum, which is a development finance institution (*attīstības finanšu institūcija*) established under the Law on Financial Development Institution that entered into force on 1 March 2015.[41]

The Latvian SOE sector is, in overall terms, comparable with many of the other post-transition economies in Eastern Europe, though when measured relative to the size of the national economy, it is larger than OECD averages (see Figure 2.4). The corporate valuation is concentrated in a few companies in the utility, network and financial sectors, as well as in a large SOE in the forestry sector (Table 2.7); this is also broadly consistent with the pattern in many East European countries.

In two aspects, Latvia is perhaps less typical. First, it is one of the relatively few post-transition governments to have wholly divested itself of all companies in the manufacturing sector. Second, there are a number of sizeable companies in the "others" category, which in most other countries would comprise mostly small-scale real estate management companies, special-purpose vehicles, etc. The reason is that the Latvian authorities have corporatized a number of public sector activities that might in other jurisdictions reside with government agencies, including the provision of public health services. The national privatisation agency is also incorporated under company law.

A few SOEs stand out in terms of individual importance. For instance, the electricity company Latvenergo is by far the most valuable corporate asset in the state portfolio, with a book equity value exceeding EUR 1.9 billion, and remains one of the largest companies headquartered in Latvia. Latvenergo enjoys a monopoly position as the largest producer of electricity in Latvia and controls all of the country's public electricity distribution networks. The next-largest SOEs are the railway company, Latvijas Dzelzceļš, which manages the public-use railway infrastructure and owns shares of Latvia's largest freight rail company, and the state forestry company, Latvijas Valsts Meži, both with an equity value just above EUR 300 million. The largest SOE employer is Latvijas Dzelzceļš, followed by Latvijas Pasts (the postal service), Latvenergo and some of the healthcare providers. A detailed list of Latvian SOEs is provided in Annex I.

The SOE ownership function is exercised in Latvia by 11 line ministries,[42] one public institution and one SOE (the Privatisation Agency).[43] Starting in mid-2015, line ministries were legally required to work with a new SOE Coordination Institution, established under the new SOE corporate governance law (see sections 2.4 and 3.3).

Figure 2.4. **Share of SOEs of total dependent employment**

Source: (1) OECD (2014), The Size and Sectoral Distribution of SOEs in OECD and Partner Countries, and (2) Latvia's responses to a standard questionnaire on its position relative to the OECD Guidelines on Corporate Governance of State-Owned Enterprises.

Table 2.7. **An overview of the companies majority-owned by the Latvian government**

Main sector	Number of enterprises	Number of employees	Value of enterprises (EUR million)
Total	**74**	**52 240**	**3 702.8**
Primary sectors	1	1 234	306.7
Manufacturing	-	-	-
Finance	5	2 230	351.3
Telecoms	5	3 138	338.7
Electricity and gas	2	4 517	2 012.6
Transportation	6	16 071	220.4
Other utilities	1	4 470	8.2
Real estate	5	960	151.1
Other activities	49	19 620	313.8

Source: OECD (2014), The Size and Sectoral Distribution of SOEs in OECD and Partner Countries, www.oecd.org/daf/ca/size-sectoral-distribution-soes-oecd-partner-countries.htm.

2.4. The Legal and Regulatory Framework for SOEs

The two most important laws in terms of SOE corporate governance are the Public Persons Capital Shares and Companies Law (PPCSCL) and the State Administration Structure Law, described in further detail below. Latvian SOEs are also subject to Latvia's CL, which governs SOEs' commercial activities except where the PPCSCL provides otherwise, as well as Latvia's accounting and auditing legal and regulatory framework. One SOE, Latvenergo, is also subject to applicable provisions under the FIML, since it has issued bonds on the Nasdaq Riga exchange.

Public Persons Capital Shares and Companies Law (PPCSCL)

On 1 January 2015, the new Latvian SOE corporate governance law, the PPCSCL, entered into force, replacing the former Law on State and Local Government Capital Shares and Capital Companies (LGCSCC). The PPCSCL outlines the responsibilities of the government as the owner of state assets, including provisions related to the oversight of corporate governance. The law sets procedures for establishing, reorganising, liquidating, or selling state-owned enterprises, as well as increasing or decreasing state shares in commercial enterprises. The law also includes provisions on the governance of state-owned and state-controlled enterprises, procedures for determining the portion of SOE profits to be paid out in dividends, and provisions on remuneration for members of SOE supervisory boards and management boards.

The PPCSCL – if effectively implemented – has the potential to address important gaps in Latvia's SOE governance framework, as identified by the Working Party in its 2014 review of Latvia's position relative to the SOE Guidelines. Importantly, the law (1) encourages the reintroduction of supervisory boards in large SOEs; (2) establishes a coordination function for Latvia's SOE sector; and (3) requires greater disclosure by SOEs and their owners, including annual aggregate reports on the sector. These provisions are summarized here and described more fully in Chapter IV. Binding implementing regulations were developed and adopted by Council at the time of writing, while non-binding implementing guidance was under development. (See Table 3.5 in section 3.3 for a full list.)

Reintroduction of SOE supervisory boards

Latvia is one of the only developed economies in the world where – as of April 2016 – most SOEs lacked supervisory boards. The supervisory boards of most Latvian SOEs were abolished in 2009[44] as a result of their politicisation. As a result, line ministries' state secretaries were required to act as the supervisory board and were individually responsible for the corporate governance and management oversight of SOEs in their ministries' portfolio. As described in the Working Party's 2014 review of Latvia's SOE corporate governance, the lack of SOE supervisory boards has exposed the SOE sector to potentially serious corporate governance failures.[45]

This departure from the SOE Guidelines remains a key area of concern for the Working Party, but one that was under reform at the time of writing. As of 1 January 2016, under the PPCSCL, large SOEs have the option to re-establish supervisory boards. "Large" SOEs are those that meet the following two PPCSCL criteria in a financial reporting year: (1) net turnover exceeding EUR 21 million and (2) balance sheet total exceeding EUR 4 million. Fifteen SOEs meet the PPCSCL's size criteria;[46] of these, the Ministry of Transport serves as the line ministry for seven; the Ministries of Finance and Health are responsible for three each; and the Ministries of Agriculture and Economy are responsible for one each. As of April 2016, the line ministries reported plans to re-establish supervisory boards in 12 of the 15 SOEs by the end of the calendar year. Three SOEs under the Ministry of Health will not establish supervisory boards, as the government has concluded that these SOEs do not operate on a commercial basis despite their legal status as LLCs.[47] (See Table 2.8.)

The option for these 12 large SOEs to re-establish boards became obligatory by end-2016 after the Latvian government adopted, on 29 March 2016, Regulation No. 235 on Establishment of Boards of Directors in State-Owned Enterprises. Further, the Latvian government agreed in April 2016 to include a legally binding commitment to implement the Working Party's recommendation to re-establish supervisory boards in at least large commercial SOEs by the end of 2016, by including it in its Final Statement accepting the obligations of OECD membership. The Final Statement will become part of the Accession Agreement with the OECD, which is an international agreement ratified by Latvia's parliament. Finally, Latvia reported to the Committee in April 2016 that, once this first round of supervisory boards are established in Latvia's largest commercial SOEs, the government may consider establishing boards in all remaining commercial SOEs, regardless of size.

Establishment of the coordination function

As noted above, Latvia's pre-PPCSCL SOE sector was decentralized, with 11 ministries[48] and one public institution and one SOE (the Privatisation Agency)[49] exercising the ownership function. This framework was changing at the time of writing, with the creation in June 2015 of a new Coordination Institution. Under the PPCSCL, the Coordination Institution's overall responsibilities are to ensure that the ownership function as exercised by line ministries and institutions is line with the PPCSCL and to more clearly separate the government's policy-making functions from ownership functions. Box 2.3 presents these responsibilities in more detail as set forth in the PPCSCL. (See also section 3.3.)

Table 2.8. **SOEs that have supervisory boards or plan to re-establish supervisory boards by end-2016**

Line Ministry		SOE	Law Regulating establishment of supervisory boards	Supervisory board established in 2016?	Status of efforts to establish a board as of July 2016
1.	Agriculture, Economy, & Finance	Development finance institution Altum	Law on Financial Development Institution	Established	–
2.	Agriculture	Latvian State Forests www.lvm.lv	PPCSCL	Established	Latvian State Forests' supervisory board was established on 11 July 2016.
3.	Economy	Latvenergo www.latvenergo.lv	PPCSCL	Expected by 30 September	Qualifications were announced and a nomination committee was established. A public call for candidates was announced on 18 July and recommendations of the nomination committee for candidates to the supervisory board will be submitted to the shareholder in September. The election of a board of directors is planned by the end of September 2016. The board will consist of five directors.
4.	Finance	High Voltage Network www.ast.lv	PPCSCL	Expected by 31 December	The ministry elaborated a description of the selection criteria of board members for JSC "Valsts nekustamie īpašumi"; a nomination committee will be established and a public call for potential candidates will be launched. After the board of directors for JSC "Valsts nekustamie īpašumi" has been elected, the ministry will move forward with the nomination procedures for JSC "Augstsprieguma tīkls" and JSC "Latvijas Loto", with the establishment of boards by the end of 2016.
5.	Finance	Latvijas Loto www.latloto.lv	PPCSCL	Expected by 31 December	
6.	Finance	Country Real Estate www.vni.lv	PPCSCL	Expected by 31 December	
7.	Health	Children Clinical University Hospital www.bkus.lv	PPCSCL	No	Despite their legal status as LLCs, Latvia's hospitals do not operate on a commercial basis. The aim of their activity is to guarantee the social right of accessible and quality healthcare services while ensuring the most rational use of public financial resources. A substantial majority of their budget derives from state funds, allocated according to agreements with the National Healthcare Service.
8.	Health	Paula Stradiņa Clinical University Hospital www.stradini.lv	PPCSCL	No	
9.	Health	Riga Eastern Clinical University Hospital www.aslimnica.lv	PPCSCL	No	
10.	Privatisation Agency	Latvian Mobile Telephone (LMT) www.lmt.lv	CL	Established	–
11.	Privatisation Agency	Lattelecom www.lattelecom.lv	CL	Established	–
12.	Privatisation Agency	Reverta www.reverta.lv	CL	Established	–

Table 2.8. **SOEs that have supervisory boards or plan to re-establish supervisory boards by end-2016** (cont.)

<table>
<tr><th></th><th>Line Ministry</th><th>SOE</th><th>Law Regulating establishment of supervisory boards</th><th>Supervisory board established in 2016?</th><th>Status of efforts to establish a board as of July 2016</th></tr>
<tr><td>13.</td><td>Transportation</td><td>Air Baltic
www.airbaltic.com</td><td>CL</td><td>Established</td><td>–</td></tr>
<tr><td>14.</td><td>Transportation</td><td>Road Safety Directorate
www.csdd.lv</td><td>PPCSCL</td><td>Expected by 31 December</td><td rowspan="7">The first round of establishment of boards seven of the Ministry of Transport's large SOEs was under way.
For the SOEs that expected to establish boards by end-May 2016:
• Latvian Road Maintenance had established a supervisory board as of 1 July 2016. This followed the establishment of a nomination committee and nomination criteria, as well as a public call for candidates that ended in early April.
• Latvian Railways' supervisory board was established on 22 July 2016. This followed the creation of a nomination committee and nomination criteria, as well as a repeated call for candidates, which closed in June.
• Latvian Post had established a supervisory board as of 1 July 2016. This followed the establishment of a nomination committee and nomination criteria, as well as a public call for candidates that ended in early April.
• Riga International Airport had established a supervisory board as of 1 July 2016. This followed the establishment of a nomination committee and nomination criteria, as well as a public call for candidates that ended in March.
• Following the first round of establishment of boards of directors, the Ministry will begin nomination procedures for the Road Safety Directorate, Passenger Train, and Latvian Air Traffic. Elections for the boards of directors for these three SOEs are planned by the end of 2016.</td></tr>
<tr><td>15.</td><td>Transportation</td><td>Latvian Road Maintenance
www.lau.lv</td><td>PPCSCL</td><td>Established</td></tr>
<tr><td>16.</td><td>Transportation</td><td>Latvian Railways
www.ldz.lv</td><td>PPCSCL</td><td>Established</td></tr>
<tr><td>17.</td><td>Transportation</td><td>Latvian Air Traffic
www.lgs.lv</td><td>PPCSCL</td><td>Expected by 31 December</td></tr>
<tr><td>18.</td><td>Transportation</td><td>Latvian Post
www.pasts.lv</td><td>PPCSCL</td><td>Established</td></tr>
<tr><td>19.</td><td>Transportation</td><td>Passenger Train
www.pv.lv</td><td>PPCSCL</td><td>Expected by 31 December</td></tr>
<tr><td>20.</td><td>Transportation</td><td>Riga International Airport
www.riga-airport.com</td><td>PPCSCL</td><td>Established</td></tr>
</table>

Source: Information provided by Latvian authorities through June 2016.

Box 2.3. **Main responsibilities of the Coordination Institution according to the Public Persons Enterprises and Capital Shares Governance Law**

The Public Persons Enterprises and Capital Shares Governance Law (PPCSCL), which was adopted on 16 October 2014 entered into force on 1 January 2015, stipulates the establishment of a Coordination Institution. The Coordination Institution's role is largely advisory. It is responsible for monitoring the performance of Latvia's SOEs and counselling the Cabinet and shareholder ministries and institutions on SOE management and corporate governance.

Art. 22 of the law sets forth the Coordination Institution's main responsibilities; these are listed below. On establishing the Coordination Institution on 1 June 2015, the Cabinet tasked it with preparing a number of the non-binding guidelines and binding regulations (requiring Cabinet approval), as described below:

- **Issuing corporate governance guidelines**: The Institution will elaborate guidelines related to the efficient governance of SOEs and state-owned shares, including, for example, guidelines for the definition of general strategic aims for state enterprise ownership (Art. 25.5) and guidelines for assessing SOE operational results (Art. 27.1).
- **Corporate governance advice**: The Institution will advise the Cabinet and line ministries and institutions on issues related to the implementation of corporate governance measures and will arrange for training of representatives from line ministries and institutions on corporate governance. These responsibilities also include recommending individuals to sit on nomination committees for nominating candidates to SOE supervisory boards (Art. 31.4).
- **Monitoring performance**: The Institution will provide line ministries and institutions with statements on the financial aims set in SOEs' medium-term operation strategy and on their financial performance (i.e. profit share paid for dividends, profit figures, return on equity, etc.), as well as the conformity of such aims with non-financial aims set in the medium-term strategy. In this capacity, the Institution can request an audit of an SOE, if deemed necessary (Art. 27.6). The Institution can also provide input, with the Ministry of Finance, on SOEs' dividend pay-out obligations set by the Cabinet (Art. 28).
- **Collect and publish SOE information**: The Institution will coordinate the publication of information on the SOE sector. This includes preparing a public website with up-to-date information on the SOE sector (i.e. turnover, assets and their value, financial efficiency and dividend payments, as well as other issues related to corporate governance) and ensuring each shareholder ministry or institution also provides this information on its own website (Art. 29). It also includes preparing an annual aggregate report on the SOE sector (Art. 30).
- **Assessment of the State's SOE portfolio**: The Institution will advise the Cabinet on any shareholder's request to obtain, maintain, or sell State shares in an enterprise. In addition, when necessary, and at least every five years, the Institution must assess the State's SOE portfolio and whether the State's enterprise ownership confirms with State-ownership laws and objectives (Art. 25).

The Coordination Institution Council

Amendments to the PPCSCL in June 2015 introduced a new advisory Coordination Institution Council (Art. 24).[50] The Council reviews and approves draft guidelines and regulations prepared by the Coordination Institution. It also makes recommendations in situations where there is disagreement between the Coordination Institution and the line ministry and/or SOE supervisory board (if one exists) over an SOE's medium-term operation strategy, or when an SOE is considering a transaction that could significantly influence its ability to meet the objectives in its operations strategy (Art. 26).

The Cabinet adopted in September 2015 a resolution that provides that the Council will be composed of representatives from eight shareholder ministries (Agriculture, Culture, Economics, Environmental Protection and Regional Development, Finance, Health, Justice, and Transport), as well as representatives from the Latvian Association of Local and Regional Governments, Latvia's Free Trade Union Confederation, and the Employers' Confederation of Latvia. (To avoid conflict of interest, line ministries involved in disputes heard by the Council may participate in, but cannot vote on or block, the Council's opinion on the considered matter.)

Annual aggregate reporting

The PPCSCL stipulates that the Coordination Institution is responsible for collecting and publishing information on the SOE sector, including the publication of an annual aggregate report and a public website (Art. 30). The PPCSCL's transitional provisions, as amended in June 2015, indicate that the Coordination Institution should submit to the Cabinet and the Saeima a first aggregate annual report under the PPCSCL in December 2015. Each year thereafter, the Coordination Institution is responsible for preparing and submitting to the Cabinet and Parliament by 30 August an annual aggregate report on Latvia's SOE sector. At the time of writing, Latvia's first aggregate report under the PPCSCL – published on 16 February 2016[51] – was the first such report since 2009, as such reports were also required under the LGCSCC but were not produced. (See also section 3.2.)

State Administration Structure Law

Latvia's SOE corporate governance legal framework also includes Latvia's rationale for state enterprise ownership, which is described in Art. 88(1) of the State Administration Structure Law[52] (SASL). On 22 October 2015, the SASL was amended to streamline the conditions under which the State may maintain or obtain ownership in commercial enterprises, reducing the number of criteria from five to three. These criteria are provided in Box 2.4.[53] The amendments to the SASL, submitted to Parliament in May 2013 as part of a broader SOE legislative reform package that included the draft PPCSCL, aim to address criticisms – including from the government itself – that the former ownership rationale may be interpreted too broadly. (See also section 3.3.)

Box 2.4. Latvia's state enterprise ownership rationale: Article 88.1, State Administration Structure Law

On 22 October 2015, the Latvian Parliament adopted amendments to Article 88.1 of the State Administration Structure Law (SASL), which expresses the State's enterprise ownership rationale. The amended SASL provision is as follows:

> *A public person may establish a capital company or obtain participation in an existing capital company in order to fulfil its functions more efficiently, unless otherwise specified by law, if one of the following conditions is met:*
>
> 1. *market deficiency - a situation where the market is incapable of ensuring protection of the public interests in respective area - is prevented;*
> 2. *operations of a capital company, of a public person, or a capital company controlled by public persons result in production of goods or services which are of strategic importance for the development of the administrative territory of the State or a local government or for national security;*
> 3. *those assets are managed which are of strategic importance for the development of administrative territory of the State or a local government or for national security.*

Notes

1. As of 2014, Russia received roughly 12% of Latvia's exports, while Latvia's large port and railway cargo transit sectors are particularly exposed to changes in Russia's economy. Latvia also receives nearly all of its natural gas from Russia. For further information, see: European Commission, *EU BOP Assistance to Latvia, Fifth Review under Post-Programme Surveillance*; IMF, *Republic of Latvia: 2014 Article IV Consultation – Staff Report; Press Release; and Statement by the Executive Director for the Republic of Latvia* (May 2014); and the December 2014 OECD Economic and Development Review of Latvia (ECO/EDR/ACS(2014)3).

2. Five Secondary List companies prepare their consolidated annual accounts according to IFRS, as required under the Financial Instruments Markets Law (see section 3.2). Three Secondary List companies have also chosen to prepare their individual accounts according to IFRS in addition to Latvian GAAP.

3. The report is also supported by information from Lursoft IT. The annual rankings are based on a calculation of normalized earnings before interest, taxes, depreciation and amortization (EBITDA); turnover; an adjustment based on 15 indicators of governance quality; and industry-specific multiples. The ranking also includes foreign-owned subsidiaries such as Swedbank (ranked 2nd) and Seb Banka (ranked 8th). See online here: www.top101.lv/en/top101/2015

4. Latvia's GDP of USD 28.2 billion in 2012 was the smallest of all the OECD countries except Estonia and Iceland, according to World Bank figures.

5. http://data.worldbank.org/indicator. Latvia's figures also lag behind those of its Baltic neighbours, with Estonia reporting 2012 market capitalisation of 10.3% and trading volume of 0.8% of GDP, and Lithuania at 9.3% market capitalisation and

0.4% trading volume. See also: Nasdaq Baltic, *Promoting Baltic Economic Growth through IPOs: Study and Action Proposals*, April 2015. (Available online here: *www.nasdaqomxbaltic.com/files/baltic/IPO_TF/Economic%20growth%20through%20IPO_EN.pdf*).

6. For up-to-date market statistics see online here: *www.nasdaqbaltic.com/market/?pg=stats&lang=en*

7. Latvian authorities report that between 2004 and 2006, 15 companies chose to de-list their shares from the regulated market under the new FIML.

8. See also: *http://west.citadele.lv/en/media-room/news/index.php?from426=2&id426=35807*.

9. The Ministry of Economics study was focused only on SMEs and did not address the issue of capital market financing, presumably because of the absence of IPOs during this period and the fact that stock exchange debt instruments have been used mainly by larger companies.

10. On 7 August 2013, the Law on Alternative Investment Funds and Managers Thereof came into force, providing unified regulation for alternative investment funds, including venture capital funds. Since then, funds and their managers have fallen under the supervision of FCMC. As of October 2014 there were 2 licensed and 6 registered fund managers, and 12 funds, under FCMC supervision.

11. The Principles of Corporate Governance refer to boards of directors as encompassing both single-tier and two-tier board systems. While the SOE Guidelines use the terminology "management" and "boards of directors" to describe the separate executive and supervisory functions in jurisdictions with two-tier systems, this report applies the term "management board" to the executive management function and the term "supervisory board" to the supervisory function (i.e. "boards of directors" under the SOE Guidelines), in order to be consistent with the terminology applied in English translations of Latvian legislation and regulations.

12. In exceptional cases, the share capital may be increased by decision of the management board (CL Art. 249.4).

13. According to a 2015 assessment of Baltic companies' compliance with regional corporate governance codes, only 6 out of Latvia's 26 listed companies (23%) follow the Nasdaq OMX Riga Principles' recommendation that at least half of the supervisory board be composed of independent directors. See: Nasdaq Baltic (2015), *Review of Corporate Governance Practices in the Baltics in 2015,* available here: *www.nasdaqbaltic.com/files/baltic/CG%20review/Review%20of%20CG%20practices%20in%20the%20Baltics%20in%202015.pdf*

14. Among these are Directive 2009/101/EC on the coordination of safeguards required by member states of companies to protect the interests of members and third parties; Directive 2012/30/EU concerning the formation of public limited liability companies and the maintenance and alteration of their capital; Directive 2012/17/EU as regards the interconnection of central, commercial and companies registers; Directive 2011/35/EU concerning mergers of public limited liability companies; Directive 82/891/EEC concerning the division of public limited liability companies; Directive 2005/56/EC on cross-border mergers of limited liability companies; Directive 2007/63/EC as regards the requirement of an independent expert's report on the occasion of merger or division of public limited liability companies; and Directive

2009/109/EC as regards reporting and documentation requirements in the case of mergers and divisions.

15. Among these are Directive 2004/39/EC on markets in financial instruments; Directive 2003/6/EC on insider dealing and market manipulation (market abuse); Directive 2003/71/EC on the prospectus to be published when securities are offered to the public or admitted to trading; Directive 2004/109/EC on the harmonisation of transparency requirements in relation to information about issuers whose securities are admitted to trading on the regulated market; Directive 2007/36/EC on the exercise of certain rights of shareholders in listed companies; and Directive 86/635/EEC on the annual accounts and consolidated accounts of banks and other financial institutions. Latvia may consider further amendments to its legal and regulatory framework to comply with recent amendments to EU Directives on Transparency (2013/50/EU of 22 October 2013), Statutory Audits (2014/56/EU of 16 April 2014), and a new Regulation on Market Abuse (Regulation No. 596/2014 of 16 April 2014), which provide member states with approximately two years to implement the new requirements.

16. A parent company is considered to have a "decisive influence" over a subsidiary if at least one of the following circumstances exists (Art. 3.3): (1) the parent company has the majority of voting rights in the dependent company; (2) the parent company has the right to appoint or remove the majority of the dependent company's members of the management board or supervisory board; (3) the parent company, exercising only its rights as a shareholder, appointed the majority of members of the management board or supervisory board; or (4) the parent company, on the basis of a shareholder agreement, has sole control of the majority of the voting rights in the dependent company.

17. The Ministry of Justice reported that most of the company group contractual agreements do not specify an amount to be paid annually to minority shareholders. The GCL's reference to compensation is a general one: Article 23 states that the amount of compensation can be determined by taking into account the profit of the company.

18. Daugavpils Lokomotivju Remonta Rupnica, a train engine and rolling stock manufacturing company, received the lowest score of 40% for its compliance with the Nasdaq Principles of Corporate Governance among 13 listed companies monitored by the Nasdaq Riga Exchange.

19. Phase 2 evaluation of Latvia's implementation of the OECD Anti-Bribery Convention, available online here: *www.oecd.org/daf/anti-bribery/latvia-oecdanti-briberyconvention.htm*.

20. Courts were able to begin suggesting mediation to disputing parties as of 1 January 2015. Mediators chosen for these mediation cases may be selected from the newly established Certified Mediators Institute.

21. Because the proposed amendments were, at the time of writing, only at the consultation stage, it is difficult to predict when the proposals will be considered by Parliament and eventually adopted. However, those provisions drafted to implement EU market abuse regulation should be implemented by July 2016 in order to meet the EU deadline. Also, as noted in section 2.1 above, the government had originally tabled for public consultation an amendment to the FIML to lower the mandatory share takeover bid threshold from 50% to 30%; however, due to market opposition to

certain aspects of these proposed amendments, the government has decided not to submit this FIML amendment to Parliament for its consideration.

22. Directive 2013/50/EU of the European Parliament and of the Council of 22 October 2013, amending (1) Directive 2004/109/EC of the European Parliament and of the Council on the harmonisation of transparency requirements in relation to information about issuers whose securities are admitted to trading on a regulated market, (2) Directive 2003/71/EC of the European Parliament and of the Council on the prospectus to be published when securities are offered to the public or admitted to trading and (3) Commission Directive 2007/14/EC laying down detailed rules for the implementation of certain provisions of Directive 2004/109/EC.

23. Regulation (EU) No 596/2014 of the European Parliament and of the Council of 16 April 2014 on market abuse (market abuse regulation), repealing Directive 2003/6/EC of the European Parliament and of the Council and Commission Directives 2003/124/EC, 2003/125/EC and 2004/72/EC.

24. No other subcommittees of the supervisory board are required under either the CL or the FIML.
Under the FIML (Art. 54), audit committees are responsible for monitoring the drawing up of the company's financial statements, monitoring the effectiveness of the company's internal control and risk management systems, monitoring the process of the statutory audit of the annual accounts, proposing an official auditor for carrying out audit services, and reviewing and monitoring the independence of the official auditor according to the independence requirements set forth under the Law on Sworn Auditors. Members of the committee are elected to three-year terms by the meeting of shareholders. The law does not set a minimum or maximum number of committee members, but it does exclude from committee membership representatives from the management board, a commercial representative of the company, as well as any executive representatives from a dependent company. The audit committee may include members of the supervisory board, but there is no requirement for any of the supervisory board members to serve on the audit committee. It must also have at least one independent member who is neither a member of the supervisory board nor the management board, and who has at least three years' of relevant experience in accounting or auditing.

25. In Latvia, the Ministry of Justice plays an important formal role in the judicial nomination process organisation, as well as, in coordination with Latvia's Judicial Council, the appointment process of Court Presidents of district (city) and regional courts. The Ministry of Justice also elaborates legal policy and the administration policy of Regional and District (city) courts, and directly oversees the administration of courts through the Court Administration. The Court Administration is responsible for drafting and implementing legal and judicial policy and strategies for the administration of first and second instance courts. It also drafts and implements the budget, manages financial and human resources, provides material and technical support and ensures data collection.

26. These requirements include semi-annual financial reporting rather than quarterly, with no obligation to follow IFRS and no obligation to report on compliance with Nasdaq corporate governance principles.

27. The IMF, Freedom House, and Council of the European Union have each published critical reports. The EU report summarised the court system as combining "several unfavourable factors such as lengthy proceedings to solve civil and commercial cases

in first instance and low clearance rates leading to a backlog of court cases. Disposition times are particularly long for insolvency proceedings." However, a more recent EU 2014 Justice Scoreboard report comparing the efficiency of judicial systems found some improvements in Latvia. See more here: IMF (*www.imf.org/external/pubs/ft/scr/2013/cr1328.pdf*); Freedom House (*www.freedomhouse.org/report/nations-transit/2014/latvia*); Council of the European Union (*ec.europa.eu/justice/effective-justice/files/cepej_study_justice_scoreboard_en.pdf*); EU 2014 Justice Scoreboard report (*http://ec.europa.eu/justice/effective-justice/files/justice_scoreboard_2014_en.pdf*).

28. *Cassation* involves examining a judgment or a decision by a lower-instance court. See *http://at.gov.lv/en/court-information/court-proceedings-in-the-supreme-court/cassation-instance*.

29. The European Commission report here relies on data from the World Bank's *Doing Business* report on Latvia, available at *www.doingbusiness.org/data/exploreeconomies/latvia/resolving-insolvency*.

30. See the Public Governance Committee's April 2015 accession assessment of Latvia in: [GOV/PGC/ACS(2015)3]. The assessment recognizes Latvia's efforts to improve its court efficiency and the capacity of the judiciary and court staff, but recommends further areas for improvement, including: defining court quality performance indicators, improving data collection and quality, and the use of client satisfaction surveys; reviewing the level of compensation and distribution of non-judicial workload between judges and court staff and reducing court staff turnover; strengthening the role of the Judicial Council and strengthening links between performance evaluation, training needs and professional development. (See pars. 150-152.)

31. See *http://financenet.tvnet.lv/nozares/150400-mantess_tranzits_pardod_latvijas_naftas_tranzita_akcijas*

32. See *www.ir.lv/2012/2/27/aivars-lembergs#s33*

33. See *www.nasdaqomxbaltic.com/market/?pg=news&news_id=245861*

34. See *http://m.pietiek.com/raksti/kugniecibas_akcionaru_sapulce_nomaina_padomi,_jau_izskan_pirmie_iebildumi*

35. See *https://newsclient.omxgroup.com/cdsPublic/viewDisclosure.action?disclosureId=477458&messageId=583173*

36. The Nasdaq Baltic Exchange has established a separate alternative market segment, First North, which has less-demanding disclosure requirements. The one Latvian company listed on First North, Baltic Telekom, is not required to submit a report on its compliance with the Nasdaq Principles.

37. For more information: *www.NASDAQomxbaltic.com/en/exchange-information/baltic-market-awards/*

38. See online here: *https://www.iosco.org/about/?subsection=mmou*

39. While this report focuses on SOEs under the control of the central government, it is worth noting that Latvia's municipalities also own or hold large shares of commercial

enterprises. As of 2012, municipalities were the sole shareholders of 323 SOEs and had decisive influence in 39 SOEs. In 243 enterprises, municipal governments held less than 50% of capital shares. The main provisions for managing and governing capital shares and capital companies owned by municipalities are similar to those for the central government: the CL and the Public Persons Capital Shares and Companies Law.

40. Under Latvia's new SOE governance law (described in section 2.4), line ministries were required to submit to the Cabinet of Ministers by 1 November 2015 an assessment of their SOE portfolio and the rationale for maintaining state enterprise ownership of each SOE and for these entities' legal status. See more in section 3.3.

41. Latvian authorities confirm that Latvia's development finance institution, Altum, is subject to the overall legal and regulatory SOE governance framework, unless there are specific provisions stipulated in the Institution's law. For example, SOE articles of association are normally adopted by the shareholder meeting prior to their submission to the Enterprise Register, but changes to Altum's articles of association require government approval.

42. These are the Ministries of Culture, Education and Science, Transport, Finance, Health, Economy, Environmental Protection and Regional Development, Interior, Welfare, Justice, and Agriculture.

43. The public institution is the National Electronic Mass Media Council, which is an independent public body. The SOE is the Latvian Privatisation Agency, which is a joint stock company owned by the Ministry of Economics.

44. Under the Law on State and Local Government Capital Shares and Capital Companies, in force until 1 January 2015, only SOEs operating as credit institutions, investment management companies, or financial institutions were required to have supervisory boards.

45. A summary of examples of past corporate governance failures involving Latvian SOEs – including Latvenergo, Air Baltic, Ventspils Nafta, and the Latvian Shipping Company – can be found in Box 7 of the Working Party's 2014 review.

46. This figure does not include the five SOEs that already have supervisory boards, in order to comply with laws other than the PPCSCL (see Table 2.8): Air Baltic (Ministry of Transport); Altum, the development finance institution (attīstības finanšu institūcija) (Ministries of Agriculture, Economy, and Finance); Lattelecom (Latvian Privatisation Agency); Latvijas Mobilais Telefons (LMT, Latvian Privatisation Agency); and Reverta (Latvian Privatisation Agency).

Readers should note that the "large" SOE size threshold in the PPCSCL differs from the definition of a "large undertaking" in the 2013 EU Accounting Directive 2013/34/EU. The Directive defines *large undertakings* as those entities whose balance sheets exceed at least two of the following three criteria in the preceding financial year: (1) balance sheet total of EUR 20 million, (2) net turnover of EUR 40 million, and (3) 250 employees. According to these new criteria, three additional SOEs could be added to the list of "large" SOEs eligible for choosing to re-establish supervisory boards, and one could be deleted. The government completed a consultation process in May 2016 on whether to amend the PPCSCL to change the "large" SOE size threshold. Following this consultation, Parliament decided in June 2016 not to change the PPCSCL size threshold.

47. The government further explained that the Ministry of Health could not, for the moment, realistically consider changing the legal status of State Hospitals from LLCs to public agencies due to ongoing loan agreements in which these hospitals have engaged to cover the expense of improving healthcare infrastructure in Latvia. Changing the hospitals' legal status prior to the completion of these loan agreements would have a serious financial impact on the hospitals and their ability to provide their State-mandated services, as well as on the State budget.

48. These are the Ministries of Culture, Education and Science, Transport, Finance, Health, Economy, Environmental Protection and Regional Development, Interior, Welfare, Justice, and Agriculture.

49. The public institution is the National Electronic Mass Media Council, which is an independent public body. The SOE is the Latvian Privatisation Agency, which is a joint stock company owned by the Ministry of Economics.

50. The PPCSCL as adopted in October 2014 provisioned for an "Advisory Council" that was responsible for advising the Coordination Institution on matters related to policy-planning and the drafting of laws on SOE corporate governance and management. The Advisory Council was not responsible for advising the Coordination Institution on its operational tasks.

51. See *www.pkc.gov.lv/468-pkc-ir-sagatavojis-p%C4%81rskatu-par-valsts-kapit%C4%81lsabiedr%C4%ABb%C4%81m-un-valstij-piedero%C5%A1aj%C4%81m-kapit%C4%81la-da%C4%BC%C4%81m-2014-gad%C4%81*

52. See *www.vvc.gov.lv/export/sites/default/docs/LRTA/Likumi/State_Administration_Structure_Law.doc*

53. Prior to the October 2015 amendments to the SASL, the five criteria justifying state enterprise ownership rationale were as follows: (1) in cases of market failure, (2) in sectors in which a natural monopoly exists, (3) in strategically important sectors, (4) in sectors that require large capital investments in order to develop, and/or (5) in sectors where higher quality standards must be met in order to protect the public interest.

References

Dreifelds, Juris, and Valts Kalninš (2014), *Latvia*, Freedom House, Washington DC, *www.freedomhouse.org/report/nations-transit/2014/latvia*.

EBRD, Commercial Laws of Latvia (2011), An Assessment by the EBRD, Office of the General Counsel, October, EBRD, London, *www.ebrd.com/downloads/sector/legal/latvia.pdf*.

European Commission Directorate-General for Justice (2015), *2015 EU Justice Scoreboard,* European Commission, Brussels, *http://ec.europa.eu/justice/effective-justice/scoreboard/index_en.htm*.

FICIL (Foreign Investors' Council in Latvia) (2015), *Position Paper on the Insolvency Process,* FICIL, Riga, www.ficil.lv/f/15%2009%2024%20Insolvency%20Process.pdf.

FICIL (2013), *Proposals for Facilitating Efficiency of the Court System*, FICIL, Riga, www.ficil.lv/view/en/22/proposals-for-facilitating-efficiency-of-the-court-system-2013.

FISIL (2011), *Position Paper on Capital Markets Development*, FICIL, Riga, *www.ficil.lv/f/11%2005%2020%20On_Capital_Markets.pdf*.

IMF (2013), *Republic of Latvia: 2012 Article IV Consultation and Second Post-Program Monitoring Discussions*, Country Report, No. 13/28, IMF, Washington DC, *www.imf.org/external/pubs/ft/scr/2013/cr1328.pdf*.

Latvia Cabinet of Ministers (2012), *Concept for Management of State Capital Shares*, Riga.

Latvia Cabinet of Ministers (2009), *Annual Review of Latvian State-Owned Assets*, Riga, p. 76.

Latvia Ministry of Economics (2015), *Economic Development of Latvia*, Ministry of Economics of the Republic of Latvia, Riga, *https://www.em.gov.lv/en/economic_development/report_on_the_economic_development_of_latvia*.

Latvia Ministry of Economics (2009), *Annual Review of Latvian State-Owned Assets*, Ministry of Economics of the Republic of Latvia, Riga.

Latvia Ministry of Justice (2014), "Court Cases Heard by the Senate (Cassation instance in the Supreme Court) 2010-2014", submission to the OECD Secretariat on 18 August 2014.

Latvia State Audit Office (2013), "Opinion: Re. 2012 Annual Report of the Republic of Latvia on the implementation of the State budget and Municipal budgets, No.5.1-2-33/2012", 13 September, Republic of Latvia State Audit Office, Riga, *www.lrvk.gov.lv/uploads/Majaslapa%20ENG/Audit%20report/2012/5.1-2-33_2012/atzinums_13092013_sgp_lav_eng-final.pdf*

Latvia State Audit Office (2015), "Is the State's Insolvency Policy Effective?", 19 March, unofficial translation, State Audit Office, Riga.

Nasdaq Baltic (2016), *Review of Corporate Governance Practices in the Baltics, www.nasdaqbaltic.com/files/baltic/CG%20review/Review%20of%20CG%20practices%20in%20the%20Baltics%20in%202015.pdf*.

Nasdaq Baltic (2015), *Promoting Baltic Economic Growth through IPOs: Study and Action Proposals, www.nasdaqbaltic.com/files/baltic/IPO_TF/0816-Q15%20Economic%20growth%20IPO_BALTIC_Eng_FNL.pdf*.

Nasdaq Baltic (2015), *Review of Corporate Governance Practices in the Baltics in 2015, www.nasdaqbaltic.com/files/baltic/CG%20review/Review%20of%20CG%20practices%20in%20the%20Baltics%20in%202015.pdf*.

Nasdaq OMX Riga (2014), *NASDAQ OMX Riga Rules on Listing and Trading of Financial Instruments on the Markets Regulated by the Exchange, www.nasdaqomxbaltic.com/files/riga/rules/NQRiga_Eng/2014_10_06_RSE_Listing_KONSOLIDETIE_T+2_ENG.pdf*.

Nasdaq OMX Riga (2010), *Principles of Corporate Governance and Recommendations on their Implementation*, www.nasdaqomxbaltic.com/files/riga/corp_gov_May_2010_final_EN.pdf.

OECD (2015a), *G20/OECD Principles of Corporate Governance*, OECD Publishing, Paris. *http://dx.doi.org/10.1787/9789264236882-en*.

OECD (2015b), *OECD Economic Surveys: Latvia 2015*, *https://www.oecd.org/eco/surveys/Overview_Latvia_2015_Eng.pdf*.

OECD (2015c), *OECD Guidelines on Corporate Governance of State-Owned Enterprises,* 2015 Edition, OECD Publishing, Paris, *http://dx.doi.org/10.1787/9789264244160-en* .

OECD (2015d), *Recommendation of the Council on Principles of Corporate Governance*, *http://acts.oecd.org/Instruments/ShowInstrumentView.aspx?InstrumentID=322&InstrumentPID=358&Lang=en&Book=False*.

OECD (2015e), *Recommendation of the Council on Guidelines on Corporate Governance of State-Owned Enterprises*, *http://acts.oecd.org/Instruments/ShowInstrumentView.aspx?InstrumentID=323&InstrumentPID=359&Lang=en&Book=False*.

OECD (2015f), *OECD Review of the Corporate Governance of State-Owned Enterprises in Latvia*, www.oecd.org/daf/ca/oecd-review-corporate-governance-soe-latvia.htm.

OECD (2014), *The Size and Sectoral Distribution of SOEs in OECD and Partner Countries*, OECD Publishing, Paris, *http://dx.doi.org/10.1787/9789264215610-en*

OECD (2013), *Roadmap for the Accession of Latvia to the OECD Convention*, *www.oecd.org/officialdocuments/publicdisplaydocumentpdf/?cote=C(2013)122/FINAL&docLanguage=En*

OECD Working Group on Bribery (2015), *Phase 2 evaluation of Latvia's implementation of the OECD Anti-Bribery Convention*, *www.oecd.org/daf/anti-bribery/Latvia-Phase-2-Report-ENG.pdf*.

World Bank (2002), Report on the Observance of Standards and Codes (ROSC): Corporate Governance Country Assessment of the Republic of Latvia, World Bank, Washington DC, *http://documents.worldbank.org/curated/en/892401468266155910/Latvia-Republic-of-Report-on-the-Observance-of-Standards-and-Codes-ROSC-Corporate-Governance-Country-Assessment*.

Chapter 3

Latvia and the core Corporate Governance Principles: The Roadmap for Accession

In 2014, Latvia was reviewed against the recommendations of the Principles of Corporate Governance and Guidelines on Corporate Governance of State-Owned Enterprises. This chapter, along with Chapter V, builds on these reviews, following the structure of the Corporate Governance Committee's "Concept Paper", which sets out five "core" corporate governance accession principles: (1) shareholder rights and equitable treatment, including treatment of the market for corporate control; (2) related party transactions and conflicts of interest (3) institutional investor disclosure, corporate governance policies, conflicts of interest and voting; (4) insider trading and abusive self-dealing; and (5) equitable treatment of shareholders among state-owned enterprises.

The 2014 review raised concerns with respect to related party transactions, the market for corporate control, and enforcement of provisions related to insider trading and market abuse. This chapter conveys reports from the Latvian authorities regarding new developments in each of these areas, and describes Latvia's recent implementation of SOE reforms.

3.1. Ensuring a consistent regulatory framework that provides for the existence and effective enforcement of shareholder rights and the equitable treatment of shareholders, including minority and foreign shareholders.

As noted in the introduction to this report, Latvia was reviewed against all of the recommendations of the *Principles of Corporate Governance* and *Guidelines on Corporate Governance of State-Owned Enterprises* in 2014. This report builds on these reviews, following the structure of the Corporate Governance Committee's *Concepts to Guide Corporate Governance Accession Reviews* ("the Concept Paper"), which provides a framework for integrating the elements most relevant to assessing each of the five "core" corporate governance accession principles. In line with the Concept Paper structure, this section therefore is divided into five sections: (1) shareholder rights and equitable treatment, including treatment of the market for corporate control (Principles II.C, D, E, and H and Principle III.B); (2) related party transactions and conflicts of interest (Principle II.F 1 and 2); (3) institutional investor disclosure, corporate governance policies, conflicts of interest and voting (Principles III.A and C); (4) insider trading and abusive self-dealing (Principle III.E); and (5) equitable treatment of shareholders among state-owned enterprises (Guidelines IV.A and C).

The 2014 review raised concerns with respect to treatment of related party transactions, developments in the market for corporate control, and enforcement of provisions related to insider trading and market abuse. The Latvian authorities have reported on new developments in each of these areas, and these are described below. There has also been some evolution with respect to SOEs due to Latvia's implementation of SOE reforms.

Shareholder rights and equitable treatment

Effective participation in general meetings

Principle II.C states that shareholders should have the opportunity to participate effectively and vote in general shareholder meetings and should be informed of the rules, including voting procedures that govern general shareholder meetings. This includes consideration of six sub-topics dealing with (1) provision of sufficient and timely information regarding general meetings; (2) processes allowing for equitable treatment of shareholders so that, for example, it is not unduly difficult or expensive to cast votes; (3) shareholders' ability to ask questions to the board and to place items on the general meeting agenda; (4) facilitation of effective participation in key corporate governance decisions such as nomination and election of board members; (5) shareholders' ability to vote in person or in absentia; and (6) the elimination of impediments to cross-border voting.

The 2014 review of Latvia against the Principles found that Latvia had CL and FIML provisions in place to address these recommendations. This includes requirements for provision of timely information **(Principle II.C.1)** through a notice on convening of the AGM to be communicated to shareholders not later than 30 days prior to the meeting – and, if the company has bearer shares, to publish the notice in the official gazette, *Latvijas Vēstnesis* (published only in electronic form at https://www.vestnesis.lv), and in at least one other newspaper. The dissemination of information on the AGM/EGM of listed companies is regulated by the FIML. In accordance with the FIML, the listed companies publish the notice on convening of the AGM/EGM on ORICGS, as well as on the website of the company and via other channels for dissemination of information. The Nasdaq Listing Rules require listed companies to disclose the regulated information in Latvian and in English, to facilitate access to information by foreign investors.

The notice on convening of the AGM/EGM must indicate the place and time of the meeting, the proposed agenda, and the place or website where shareholders may become acquainted with the draft resolutions and other issues included in the agenda. The notice should also include information on activities which must be conducted by the shareholder before the meeting in order to be able to participate and vote at the meeting and the information on the participation of representatives of shareholders at the meeting. In addition, the listed companies have a duty to stipulate the rights of shareholders to put items on the agenda, to submit draft resolutions for discussion, and ask questions about the items on the agenda and the deadline by which these rights may be exercised.

Within 30 days before the AGM/EGM, taking into account the information publication deadlines laid down in law, the listed companies have to ensure that draft resolutions or explanations regarding the items on the agenda where no resolutions are taken are available on the website of the company. The forms to be used to vote by proxy should also be made available on the website of a listed company. The listed companies are also obliged to submit the draft resolutions to the ORICGS not later than 14 days prior to the AGM/EGM. Additionally, the Nasdaq Listing Rules stipulate that the listed companies are deemed to have disclosed the draft resolutions if they provide sufficient information for a shareholder to decide on his/her vote on the agenda item in question. The Nasdaq Principles recommend that listed companies ensure that the shareholders may get acquainted with the whole texts of draft resolutions, especially if they apply to voting on amendments to the company's statutes, election of the supervisory board members, determination of their remuneration, distribution of the company's profit and other significant issues (26 of 29 listed companies reported fully implementing this recommendation).

Measures in place to allow shareholders to participate at the AGM/EGM (either in person or through a representative via written proxy authorization) and related provisions would appear to address the recommendations of **Principles II.C.2** and **II.C.5**. The FIML contains provisions that enable listed companies through their articles of association (AoA) to establish provisions for shareholders to vote electronically. These provisions appear to be consistent with the recommendation to not make it unduly difficult or expensive to cast votes (though this was not possible to verify on an individual company basis).

Principle II.C.3 calls for shareholders to have the opportunity to submit questions to the board and to place items on the agenda, subject to reasonable limitations. This appears to have been addressed through CL and FIML provisions that allow shareholders who jointly represent not less than 1/20 of the equity capital to have the right to request inclusion of additional issues on the agenda of the AGM/EGM and to submit additional draft resolutions for the items on the agenda of the meeting.

The report also concluded that legal provisions are in place to facilitate effective shareholder participation in key corporate governance decisions such as the nomination and election of board members (**Principle II.C.4).** In accordance with the CL, the AGM/EGM elects, re-elects and recalls the supervisory board members, as well as determines the general principles, types and criteria of remuneration intended for the management and supervisory board members. The AGM/EGM also determines the specific amount of remuneration for each supervisory board member.

Shareholders are entitled to nominate their candidates for election of the supervisory members. The candidates may be nominated by a shareholder or a group of shareholders. However, each of the candidates must have support from not less than 5% of the capital with voting rights represented at the AGM/EGM. Thus, even a minority shareholder is entitled to nominate a candidate.

In accordance with the CL and the FIML, shareholders must receive information on the supervisory board candidates at least 14 days before the AGM/EGM. The Nasdaq Principles also invite the listed companies to ensure that the candidates participate at the AGM/EGM, so the shareholders are able to ask the candidates questions. However, reasonable restrictions on questions may be set; for example, excluding the possibility that one shareholder can use up the total time provided for asking the questions, or setting a time limit for speeches. This recommendation was reported as fully implemented by 24 of 29 listed companies.

Finally, the 2014 report also found no legal impediments to cross-border voting **(Principle II.C.6),** consistent with the related measures already described above. Forms for proxy voting must be made available on company websites 30 days before the AGM, voting by mail is permitted if the votes are submitted before the meeting, and electronic voting may be used if permitted under the company's AoA, as described in Principle II.C.4. No legal impediments to cross-border voting were identified.

Shareholder consultation and coordination in the exercise of their rights

Principle II.D states that shareholders, including institutional shareholders, should be allowed to consult with each other on issues concerning their basic shareholder rights as defined in the Principles, subject to exceptions to prevent abuse. As noted in the 2014 review of Latvia, the CL and the FIML neither restrict nor promote co-operation and coordination among shareholders. However, actions of shareholders acting in concert may trigger the rules for a mandatory share buyout offer.

The Nasdaq Principles support consultations among shareholders during the AGM/EGM if it is required in order to take a decision or to achieve clarity on some issue; all but one of the listed companies reported fully complying with this recommendation, and the remaining company reported partial compliance with an explanation).

Equal treatment with respect to different share classes

Principle II.E states that all shareholders of the same series of a class should be treated equally. Capital structures and arrangements that enable certain shareholders to obtain a degree of influence or control disproportionate to their equity ownership should be disclosed.

The CL permits companies to issue shares with different rights. However, in practice, all shares of the main list companies are voting shares, and only three of the 25 secondary list companies have non-voting shares – and these represent just 0.3% of the total amount of shares in these three companies, according to the Latvian self-evaluation.[1]

The CL stipulates that rights attached to different categories of shares may differ in respect to receiving dividends, receiving a liquidation quota or exercising the voting rights at the AGM/EGM. However, in accordance with Art. 54 of the FIML, the management board is responsible for ensuring equal treatment of all shareholders that own shares of the same category. Furthermore, the management board has a duty to provide shareholders with information on any changes in the rights attached to various categories of the company's shares.

If a company has issued several categories of shares, it must conform to special voting procedures regarding the increase or reduction of the equity capital and changes in the rights of shareholders of a particular category of shares. Such decisions may be taken at the AGM/EGM, if shareholders of each of the relevant categories of shares vote for it in each group of shareholders, by a majority of votes of the shareholders with voting rights present as laid down in law or the AoA.

Transparency of the market for corporate control

A second sub-recommendation under Principle II.E calls for the mandatory disclosure of capital structures and control arrangements. This is also relevant to assessing Latvia against **Principle II.H**, which recommends that the market for corporate control be allowed to function in an efficient and transparent manner.

The 2014 review of Latvia noted some concerns with respect to the transparency of the Latvian market for corporate control and the enforcement of automatic takeover bids. In accordance with the FIML, a mandatory offer to buy out the shares belonging to other shareholders must be made by a person or persons acting in concert acquiring directly or indirectly 50% or more of the voting rights attached to the company's shares. A mandatory share buyout offer must be made also in the case of de-listing the company.

The FIML also provides for protection of the rights of minority shareholders in case there is a shareholder who directly or indirectly owns 90% or more of the shares of a listed company. Minority shareholders are entitled, until the time when a final share buyout offer is made, to request that this person buys out their shares. The buyout price of shares is determined in accordance with the provisions of the FIML.

In practice, there have been several documented cases in which shareholders have exceeded the 50% threshold but have not made mandatory buyout offers. The FCMC has pursued enforcement actions (including two administrative fines in 2009, for EUR 7 100 and EUR 8 500, issued to companies for failing to make such offers, and similar fines for cases that occurred in 2003 and 2007), but the shareholders subsequently sold the shares that placed them over the 50% threshold so that they would not have to make a mandatory offer. In one administrative case in August, 2014, the FCMC issued two fines of EUR 14 200 each against two persons acting in concert to violate the 50% threshold. Again in this case, the shareholders involved reduced their shares back to below 50% before the sanction was issued, eliminating the requirement for a mandatory share takeover bid.[2] In November 2014, the FCMC issued two fines – EUR 14 200 and EUR 10 650 – against two shareholders acting in concert to violate the 50% threshold. Both of these FCMC decisions were appealed in court.

The 2014 OECD review of Latvia concluded that because some shareholders typically do not participate in the AGM and – due to the ease with which the largest shareholder may be able to act in concert with smaller shareholders whose ownership is not disclosed below the 5% threshold – the actual threshold for achieving effective control is likely to be well below the 50% threshold. Lowering the threshold could help to reduce the potential for controlling shareholders to abuse this provision, and could also increase liquidity in the market by lowering the maximum threshold under which a single shareholder or shareholders acting in concert can exercise ownership in a company. The report therefore concluded that lowering the threshold for mandatory share buyouts below 50% could be considered, among other measures, to strengthen minority shareholder rights.

As noted above, the government recently tabled a consultation draft of amendments to the FIML that included a proposal to lower the mandatory share buyout threshold from 50% to 30%. The amendments lowering the threshold to 30% were adopted and entered into force on 29 June 2016. According to the FIML amendments, they establish a certain range of persons that, *per se*, shall be regarded as persons acting in concert, unless they provide for the contrary. The burden of proof is put on the persons possibly acting in concert. Existing shareholders who had launched a mandatory bid under the former threshold of 50% are exempt from the new regulation. Shareholders with an ownership stake of between 30 percent and 50 percent are to launch a mandatory share buyout bid if their ownership stake increases.

Principle II.H.2 further states that anti-takeover devices should not be used to shield management and the board from accountability. In accordance with the FIML, the management and supervisory board members of the target company are prohibited from interfering with a share buyout offer by taking action or refraining from any action.

In case of a voluntary share buyout, the management and supervisory boards must acquire prior authorization of the AGM/EGM for carrying out activities that may frustrate the success of the buyout offer. This obligation is in effect from the moment when the offerer notifies the management and supervisory boards of a target company regarding its intention to make a voluntary share buyout offer until the expiration date of the offer. Such authorization is not necessary where alternative share buyout offers are sought.

A last area for consideration of the treatment of shareholders in this section is **Principle III.B** which states that votes should be cast by custodians or nominees in line with the directions of the beneficial owner of the shares. Data on the actual practical application of this recommendation was not available, but the Latvian authorities reported that investment brokerage companies and credit institutions must sign a written contract with the customer prior to providing investment services and ancillary (non-core) investment services. The contract must stipulate the procedures for information exchange on events regarding financial instruments (e.g. a meeting of shareholders, payment of dividends and interest, redemption of debt financial instruments, changing the nominal value of financial instruments, uniting issues of financial instruments, dividing issues of financial instruments, issuing subscription rights).

Related Party Transactions and Conflicts of Interest

Principle II.F states that related party transactions should be approved and conducted in a manner that ensures proper management of conflicts of interest and protects the interests of the company and its shareholders. (1) Conflicts of interest inherent in related-party transactions should be addressed; and (2) members of the board and key executives should be required to disclose to the board whether they, directly, indirectly or on behalf of third parties, have a material interest in any transaction or matter directly affecting the corporation.

Framework for supervision of related party transactions

The Committee, in its 2014 assessment of Latvia's position relative to the OECD Principles of Corporate Governance, identified gaps in Latvia's related party transactions framework as an area of concern. The Committee's concern was underpinned by the emphasis placed by representatives from the private sector on the importance of enforcing provisions on the supervision and disclosure of related party transactions, particularly in a small country like Latvia. One listed company representative explained to the OECD

Secretariat, for example, that there have been a number of recent high-profile cases where companies have "gone bust" because of serious breaches of related party transaction provisions. (One example includes the aforementioned insolvent Liepajas Metalurgs, whose demise was allegedly due in part to abusive related party transactions.) This section focuses, first, on the framework for guiding the supervisory board's supervision of related party transactions. The framework for disclosing related party transactions is discussed further in section 3.2.

Specifically, the Corporate Governance Committee's concerns relate to the *definition* of related party transactions under Latvian law. Art. 139^3 of the CL requires the supervisory board's approval of related party transactions. Article 139^1 of the CL defines "related party" as follows:

> *a person who is a relative of the founder of the company, shareholder, member of the [management] board...or council up to the second degree of kinship, the spouse or brother-in-law or sister-in-law up to the first degree of affinity, or a person with whom he or she has a shared household;*
>
> *another commercial company, in which the majority of shares of a capital company or investment (capital) shares of a partnership belong to the relevant founder, shareholder, member of the board...or council;*
>
> *another capital company, in which the relevant founder, shareholder, member of the [management] board...or council is a member of the [management] board...or council.*

This definition, which applies to the board's *supervision* of related party transactions, is narrower than the definition of a "related party" that is applied for the purposes of *disclosing* related party transactions, which is provided under the Art. 1.3 of the Annual Accounts and Consolidated Annual Accounts Law, in that CL Art. 139^1 does not include *indirect* ownership or control of another entity via intermediaries.[3] It was the Corporate Governance Committee's assessment in 2014 that the differing definitions may create some risk of a disconnect or confusion between what is sufficiently important for the board to review and decide upon, versus the larger universe of transactions that must be disclosed to be consistent with international standards.

Separate from, but related to, the definition of related party transactions are the *procedures* for approving related party transactions. The provisions in force at the time of writing are provided under Arts. 139^2 and 139^3 of the CL for transactions involving members of the supervisory board or management board or related persons, and under Arts. 211 and 280 for transactions involving shareholders or related persons. Art. 139^2 covers cases where a company, within two years of its establishment (or longer if specified in the articles of association), concludes a transaction with the founder, shareholder or related person regarding the acquisition of property, whose value exceeds 1/10 of the equity capital of the company. In these specific cases, the transaction must be approved by the meeting of shareholders. Art. 139^3 covers all other cases in which a company concludes a transaction with a member of the management board, the supervisory board, or a related person. In these cases, the supervisory board shall approve the transaction. Notably, the audit committee has no statutory role with respect to review of related party transactions.

In cases of conflict of interest of a member of the supervisory board, that member shall not have voting rights, and this shall be entered into the minutes of the supervisory board meeting. This abstention also applies to supervisory board members related to the supervisory board member considered to have a conflict of interest. In cases where no members of the board have voting rights, the transaction shall be approved by the meeting of shareholders. Finally, shareholders must abstain from voting if a decision is to be taken regarding conclusion of a transaction with him or her, or a related person, as per Art. 211.2.3 (limited liability companies) and Art. 280.2.5 (joint-stock companies).

The Nasdaq Principles also recommend individual members of supervisory boards of listed companies to avoid any supposed or actual conflicts of interest (Principle 8.1). Under Principle 8.2, directors must notify other board members without delay if there is – or may be – a conflict of interest regarding any deal or agreement the company is planning to conclude with a person who has a close relationship with, or is connected to, the director in question. Directors should also disclose to the board any conflicts of interest during the validity period of concluded agreements. Under Principle 8.3, directors should excuse themselves from voting on decisions where there could be a potential conflict of interest.

To address concerns raised by the Corporate Governance Committee and to prepare for the adoption of the Council of the European Union's Proposal for the Amendments to the Shareholders Rights Directive,[4] Latvia's Ministry of Justice undertook a review in 2015 of its framework for reviewing, approving, and disclosing related party transactions. As part of this review, the Ministry identified several shortcomings in the framework vis-à-vis the Proposal that would require amendments to Latvia's laws and regulations. Latvian authorities reported at the time that changes to Latvia's framework could include: broadening Latvia's definition of "related party", defining *materiality*, requiring disclosure of material related party transactions prior to their conclusion, and reviewing CL provisions on board approval of related party transactions. Changes could also include allowing audit committees to prepare a report on material related party transactions.

In December 2015, the Ministry of Justice's longstanding multi-stakeholder working group decided to commence discussions on how to improve the framework for the review, approval and disclosure of related party transactions. As of March 2016, the working group had agreed on an initial set of proposals for public consultation; these are summarised in Box 3.1 below. The Ministry of Justice, which leads the working group, reported it plans to submit draft legislative amendments to Latvia's related party transaction framework to Parliament for review in its autumn session, starting in September 2016.

Box 3.1. Preliminary proposals to amend the framework for reviewing, approving, and disclosing related party transactions

1. **A new definition of a "related party" in the Financial Instruments Market Law (FIML).** The term "related party" will have the same meaning as in the international accounting standard adopted in accordance with Regulation (EC) No 1606/2002 of the European Parliament and of the Council (International Accounting Standard 24) and already included in the Annual Accounts and Consolidated Annual Accounts Law (see section 3.2 below);
2. **A clarification of types of related party transactions (RPTs) and a definition of materiality in the FIML.** Proposed amendments would distinguish between two kinds of related party transactions: "non-routine RPTs" and "RPTs of a significant amount or material routine RPTs". The former include transactions not concluded within the scope of ordinary business operations of the company, or which are not concluded on normal market terms; the latter include material RPTs. In these cases, "material" is defined as a transaction, which amounts to at least 10% of the company's equity according to the latest audited annual accounts or consolidated annual accounts (if prepared). If several transactions with the same related-party are concluded within any 12-month period, they should be aggregated for the purpose of determining materiality.
3. A requirement that all related party transactions:
   - **Be immediately disclosed.** Under proposed amendments to the FIML, information on related party transactions (including information on the nature of the related party relationship, the name of the related party, the value of the transaction, and the impact of the transaction on business and financial results of the company) and the audit committee's or expert's opinion (if any were required) must be disclosed..
   - **Be approved by the supervisory board or shareholder meeting.** Under proposed amendments to the Commercial Law, RPTs must be approved by the supervisory board or the meeting of shareholders. The abstention of related supervisory board members would be mandatory; if all members of the supervisory board are regarded as related ones, a transaction must be approved by the shareholder meeting;
4. **An option for the supervisory board of a company to ask the audit committee or other expert to give its opinion on the RPT.** The opinion of the audit committee or the expert must be disclosed in accordance with the FIML.

Source: Information provided by the Latvian authorities as of March 2016.

Framework for disclosing conflicts of interest

The 2014 review did not identify similar concerns with respect to **Principle II.F.2**'s recommendation that board members be required to disclose their interests in material transactions. A transaction between a company and its management or supervisory board member, or a person related to him or her, must be approved by the management and supervisory boards under the CL. If a management or supervisory board member has a material interest in the transaction, the management or supervisory board member is deprived of voting rights in the matter, and it is entered in the minutes of the management/supervisory board meeting. The management or supervisory board member is obliged to notify of such interests before the beginning of the meeting.

In addition, listed companies are required in accordance with the FIML to disclose information on the number of the shares with voting rights belonging to management and supervisory board members. Management and supervisory board members, key officials and persons related to them have a duty to make a notice of transactions in the company's shares or in financial instruments linked to such shares and submit this notification to the FCMC.

Institutional investor disclosure, corporate governance policies, conflicts of interest and voting

Principle III.A (formerly Principle II.F.1) states that "Institutional investors acting in a fiduciary capacity should disclose their corporate governance and voting policies with respect to their investments, including the procedures that they have in place for deciding on the use of their voting rights."

As noted in Chapter III, institutional investors do not tend to be active in Latvian equity markets, and in many cases individuals or companies are the main, controlling shareholders of listed companies. Nevertheless, Latvian legislation does provide for institutional investors to disclose investment and voting policies as well as some relevant elements of corporate governance policies.

The Law on Private Pension Funds requires the management board of a pension fund to prepare an investment policy. The investment policy must determine the principles for investing the pension scheme assets, the methods for determining the risks related to investments, and the risk management system. The investment policy must also include a description of the voting policy in relation to investments, which allows participation in decision-making regarding investments. Moreover, the description of the voting policy must stipulate the procedures for decision-making regarding the use of the voting rights. The investment policy should also be published on the website of the pension fund.

The Law on Private Pension Funds further stipulates that the management board of a pension fund must ensure the creation of a corresponding reporting and control system in order to ascertain that the fund manager manages the funds of the pension scheme in accordance with the policy and procedures laid down by the management board of the pension fund.

The Law on Investment Management Companies requires an investment management company to draw up the procedures for exercising the voting rights arising from the financial instruments in the fund investment portfolio. These procedures should determine the activities necessary in order to supervise and ensure the exercising of the voting rights. In addition, the procedures should prevent or manage all conflicts of interest arising from the exercising of the voting rights. An investment management company must publish a brief summary of the procedure on its website. Additionally, upon request the company should inform the fund investors free of charge regarding any activities carried out on the basis of that procedure.

Principle III.C (formerly Principle II.F.2) states that institutional investors acting in a fiduciary capacity should disclose how they manage material conflicts of interest that may affect the exercise of key ownership rights regarding their investments.

The Law on Private Pension Funds imposes a duty on pension funds to draw up a policy for preventing situations involving conflicts of interests. The policy must ensure timely identification and management of potential conflict of interest situations. It must include actions of employees for the prevention of a situation of a conflict of interests. The policy should also indicate that the conditions for transactions are not in contradiction with the pension scheme and the interests of its participants.

Information on the prevention of potential conflicts of interests must be included in the investment policy of a pension fund as well. The investment policy must indicate how the pension fund will ensure that, in case of a potential conflict of interest, the manager of funds invests the pension scheme assets only in the interests of participants of the pension scheme. The pension fund must ensure that the investment policy of the fund is available to participants of the pension scheme and also must publish it on the fund's website.

In accordance with the provisions of the Law on Investment Management Companies, investment management companies also have a duty to draw up a policy for the prevention of conflicts of interest. The policy should identify the circumstances that (1) give rise or might give rise to a conflict of interest or (2) create material threat or harm to the fund or interests of one or several clients in relation to the management services provided by the company or a third party on the company's behalf. In addition, the policy should determine the procedures and measures necessary for the prevention of conflicts of interests. The same is attributable to alternative investment fund managers, in accordance with the Law on Alternative Investment Funds and Managers Thereof.

Insider trading and abusive self-dealing

Principle III.E states that insider trading and market manipulation should be prohibited and the applicable rules enforced.

As noted, the 2014 review of Latvia raised some concerns with respect to the effectiveness of Latvia's enforcement framework against insider trading and other market abuse. Specifically, the review highlighted the low level of enforcement activity under FIML and Criminal Law provisions against insider trading and other forms of market abuse, the lack of cooperation between the FCMC and the State Police on economic crimes, and the absence of actual administrative and criminal sanctions for this behaviour. (See also section 2.2 above on overall enforcement under the FIML.)

Under the legal framework currently in force, insider trading and other forms of market manipulation are prohibited under Chapter VI of the FIML, which applies to both natural and legal persons. Under FIML Art. 148 (liability under the FIML), the FCMC is entitled to warn an issuer and/or impose a fine of up to EUR 14 200. (Fines against investment brokerages and credit institutions are higher, at EUR 142 300.) Section 193 of the Criminal Law establishes a criminal offence for "illegal activities with financial instruments and means of payment" in situations where "substantial harm has been caused by the commission thereof". The offence provides for a maximum prison term of ten years for natural persons, or a maximum fine of 200 times the minimum monthly wage, with or without the confiscation of property. If the offence is committed on a large scale, or if it is committed in an organised group,[5] then the prison sentence is 5 to 15 years with confiscation of property. Finally, the FIML requires that inside information be disclosed on ORICGS. Nasdaq Riga Listing Rule 13.2 further requires that inside information also be disclosed to the Exchange.

As noted above, the FCMC's enforcement of the FIML provisions against insider trading and market manipulation has been low, and cooperation with the State Police on allegations of serious economic crime under the Criminal Law has been very limited. At the time of writing, the FCMC, the Ministry of Justice and State Police were reviewing their legal framework and practices in the context of the new EU Regulation on Market Abuse, which should be implemented by EU member countries by July 2016. As part of this effort, the FCMC proposed amendments to the FIML to increase administrative sanctions against natural and legal persons for insider trading and market abuse. These amendments were submitted to Parliament for review in February 2016, adopted on 26 June 2016 and entered into force on 29 June 2016. Parallel amendments proposed by the Ministry of Justice to Section 193 of the Criminal Law were adopted on 1 January 2016 for entry into force on 1 March 2016. (For a full description of these amendments see section 2.2 above.). In addition to these legal reforms, the FCMC and the State Police have indicated a willingness to cooperate more closely in the detection and investigation of economic crimes. As a first step in this direction, they organized an information-sharing seminar in October 2015. (See also section 2.2 on enforcement of Latvia's corporate governance framework.)

Although such reforms would provide welcome greater flexibility to intervene more directly in such cases, successful prosecution at the criminal level would be likely to have a greater impact, as a stronger deterrent to such practices.

Equitable treatment of shareholders among state-owned enterprises

Shareholder protections (Guideline IV.A)

Guideline IV.A provides that the state should strive toward full implementation of the *OECD Principles of Corporate Governance* when it is not the sole owner of SOEs, and of all relevant sections when it is the sole owner of SOEs. This includes the following shareholder protections: (1) The state and SOEs should ensure that all shareholders are treated equitably; (2) SOEs should observe a high degree of transparency, including (as a general rule) equal and simultaneously disclosure of information, towards all shareholders; (3) SOEs should develop an active policy of communication and consultation with all shareholders; (4) the participation of minority shareholders in shareholder meetings should be facilitated so they can take part in fundamental corporate decisions, such as board elections; and (5) transactions between the state and SOEs, and between SOEs, should take place on market consistent terms.

Ensuring equitable treatment (Guideline IV.A.1): SOEs in Latvia are subject to the CL's requirement for equal treatment of all shareholders, including minority non-state shareholders in SOEs (Art. 226). Non-state shareholders are guaranteed, by law, non-discrimination, access to information, and access to voting in shareholder meetings. The State is equal to all other shareholders. In addition, the State does not have access to priority shares (i.e. "golden shares"). One share or stock equals one vote.

The treatment of non-state shareholders rights is further regulated by shareholder agreements in companies whose shareholders include outside investors and strategic partners, such as Lattelecom and – prior to the completion of the sale of state shares in April 2015 – Citadele. (In both of these companies, there were only two shareholders.) In unlisted companies, the details of shareholder agreements are confidential. Technically, this runs counter to the recommendations of the Guidelines, although where the non-state shareholders are all parties to the shareholder agreements, issues of minority protection do not in practice arise.[6]

Transparency toward all shareholders (Guideline IV.A.2): Latvia's SOEs are subject to Art. 194 of the CL, which states shareholders "have the right to receive information from the management board regarding the activities of the company and to become acquainted with all of the company's documents." The right for all shareholders to receive information from the management board may be restricted by a decision of a meeting of shareholders "if there is a justified suspicion that the shareholder may use the information acquired in contradiction to the aims of the company, and thus causing significant harm or losses to the company."

Information-sharing between the state shareholder representative (normally state secretaries or deputy state secretaries) and the line ministries may be restricted under CL Art. 19, which allows a company to classify certain "economic, technical, or scientific" matters as commercial secrets, and Art. 5.2.3 of the Freedom of Information Law, which could be interpreted to restrict the sharing of commercial secrets between state secretaries and other individuals (i.e. the minister) of an SOE's line ministry.[7] Latvia stated that state secretaries would not share commercial secrets with "third parties", but did not specifically clarify at the OECD Secretariat's request whether commercial secrets would be shared with individuals in the responsible ministry, particularly the minister.

Communication and consultation with shareholders (Guideline IV.A.3): Latvia's SOEs are also subject to CL provisions requiring management boards notify shareholders and an auditor of upcoming shareholder meetings.[8] The person who initiates the convening of the meeting – usually the chair of the management board – is responsible for ensuring that shareholders and the auditor receive draft decisions and other materials not later than three days before the meeting.

Latvian authorities provide as an example of shareholder communication and consultation Air Baltic's efforts to ensure that information is available to all shareholders (including non-state shareholders).[9] This includes notice of the convening of a shareholders' meeting, announced not later than 30 days before the planned meeting, with details on the meeting time, agenda, and voting decisions to be taken, as well as points of contact for shareholders' questions on arrangements for the meeting and agenda issues. Air Baltic shareholders may also request copies of draft decisions free of charge up to 14 days before the announced shareholder meeting and may request the management board to submit information to the shareholder meeting on the company's economic situation. Another example provided by the Latvian authorities is the publication on Reverta's website of governance and shareholder meetings, in order to enable the participation of all shareholders in shareholder meetings.[10]

Minority shareholders' participation (Guideline IV.A.4): Latvian authorities state that minority shareholder participation is facilitated in SOE shareholder meetings under the CL, which allows shareholders to participate in a shareholder meeting through a representative who has written authorisation.[11] Shareholder meeting minutes must include reference to the shareholder's representation via proxy. Special authorisation in this case is also not necessary for a person who represents the shareholder on the basis of law.

There are few SOEs in Latvia with non-state shareholders, but Latvian authorities report that participation in meetings of shareholders organized by SOEs with non-state shareholders has been generally high. For example, TILTS Communications is involved in Lattelecom shareholder meetings,[12] and EBRD is involved in shareholder meetings at

Reverta, and was involved in shareholder meetings at Citadele. (The Latvian authorities note that non-state shareholders other than EBRD do not regularly participate in Reverta shareholder meetings.) Similarly, The Ministry of Transport also confirmed that the natural persons holding 0.23% of shares in Air Baltic participate in the company's annual shareholder meeting.

Transactions between the state and SOEs and between SOEs (Guideline IV.A.5): Annotations to this Guideline note that this recommendation is "conceptually related to the issue of abusive related party transactions" and advises governments "to ensure the market consistency of all transactions by SOEs with the state and state-controlled entities". Latvian authorities explain that "SOEs are not engaged in substantial related party transactions or [in] providing each other [with] commercial loans." Latvia further stated that business and commercial transactions that do take place between SOEs are based on purely commercial grounds and are carried out in compliance with general market principles. (See section 3.2 for further discussion of SOEs' requirements to report on transactions with related entities.)

Disclosure of public policy objectives (Guideline IV.C)

Guideline IV.C states that, where SOEs are required to pursue public policy objectives, adequate information about these should be available to non-state shareholders at all times. Prior to the entry into force of the PPCSCL, there were no legal requirements for Latvian SOEs to disclose information on the fulfilment of social or public policy objectives. The PPCSCL includes new provisions on the disclosure of financial and non-financial information by individual SOEs and the SOE sector as a whole, discussed more fully below (see section 3.2 and 3.3).

3.2. Requiring timely and reliable disclosure of corporate information in accordance with internationally recognised standards of accounting, auditing and non-financial reporting.

This section focuses on three main areas: accounting and auditing standards (Principles V.B and C and Guidelines VI.A, B, and C); disclosure of governance, ownership, and voting structures (Principles II.E.2, V.A.3 and V.A.9 and Guideline VI.A.3); and disclosure of related party transactions (Principle V.A.6 and Guideline VI.A.8).

Accounting and auditing standards

Accounting standards (Principle V.B and Guideline VI.A)

Principle V.B recommends that information should be prepared and disclosed in accordance with high quality standards of accounting and financial and non-financial reporting. In Latvia, the general accounting framework is set forth in the Law on Accounting. Art. 2 of the Law on Accounting requires an entity to organise its accounts to clearly reflect all economic transactions and in a way that would allow a third person qualified in the area of accounting to obtain a true and clear representation of the entity's financial position at the date of the balance sheet, the results of the activities thereof, the cash flow for a specific time period, as well as the beginning of each economic transaction and its course. Accounts should be truthful, comparable, timely, significant, understandable and complete.

The application of financial and non-financial reporting standards is determined under the new Annual Accounts and Consolidated Annual Accounts Law (adopted 22 October 2015),[13] regulations of the FCMC, and the FIML. Under these laws, two sets of financial reporting standards may apply to the preparation of annual accounts: International Financial Reporting Standards (IFRS) and Latvian Generally Accepted Accounting Principles (Latvian GAAP). A summary of which standards apply to which companies is included in Box 3.2.

Box 3.2. **Financial reporting standards requirements under Latvian law**

In Latvia, the requirements for how companies prepare their annual and consolidated annual reports are set forth in the October 2015 Annual Accounts and Consolidated Annual Accounts Law, the Financial Instruments Market Law and FCMC regulations, which are complemented by the Nasdaq Riga Listing Rules for listed companies.

Under the Annual Accounts and Consolidated Annual Accounts Law (entered into force 1 January 2016):

- Individual, non-listed companies must apply Latvian GAAP when preparing annual accounts.
- Large SOEs may prepare their individual annual accounts using IFRS (Art. 3.7).
- Non-listed companies in a "company group situation" (i.e. the company has controlling influence over one or more other companies) *may* apply IFRS to consolidated annual reports (Art. 70).

FIML and FCMC regulations

- All companies that are listed on the main list *must* prepare their individual annual accounts using IFRS (FIML Art. 56.3). Companies that are in a company group situation and listed on the main list must also prepare their consolidated annual accounts using IFRS (FIML Art. 56.2).
- Secondary list companies shall prepare their individual annual accounts in accordance with Latvian GAAP for their individual accounts. However, the FCMC reports that, in practice, 3 issuers (out of 21) from the secondary list have chosen to voluntarily apply IFRS in addition to Latvian GAAP in the preparation of their financial accounts.
- In accordance with FCMC regulations, financial institutions (including companies whose stock is listed on the secondary list) must prepare their annual accounts (individual and consolidated annual accounts) according to IFRS.

Nasdaq Riga listing rules

- Companies on the bond list *must* apply IFRS to the preparation of their financial statements (individual annual accounts) under the Nasdaq Riga Listing Rules (Section 7, Art. 7.2 and 7.3; Section 14, Art. 14.8).

Source: Information provided by the Latvian authorities as of October 2015.

A distinction is made in this report between Latvian GAAP and IFRS because of concerns, in particular in relation to rules for transparency and disclosure by SOEs, that Latvian GAAP may not require the same level of disclosure as IFRS. This is an assessment expressed both by representatives of LASA and by the Latvian government and highlighted as an area of concern by the Working Party during its 2014 assessment of Latvia's SOE governance framework. In its 2009 review of the application of Latvian

GAAP by some Latvian SOEs, for example, the government stated that Latvian GAAP is "similar to IFRS, however certain differences exist that might affect the valuation of assets and liabilities. Latvian reporting standards have significantly lower requirements for the disclosure of financial information."[14] LASA and Latvian authorities also explain that additional differences relate to the treatment of taxes, leases, share-based payments, post-employment benefits, value measurement and the definition of financial instruments.[15]

As a result of these assessments, the Working Party recommended in 2014 that Latvia require at least large SOEs to prepare their annual and consolidated annual reports according to IFRS. In response, Latvia included a new provision in the Annual Accounts and Consolidated Annual Accounts Law (Art. 3.7) that does not require large SOEs to apply IFRS, but gives them the option to apply IFRS to individual and consolidated annual reports.[16, 17] This provision, which falls short of the Working Party recommendation, applies to annual and consolidated annual accounts starting with the financial year 2016. Immediately after this provision's entry into force on 1 January 2016, the Latvian government indicated that only eight of Latvia's 15 largest SOEs were either already applying IFRS or would choose to apply IFRS under the new Annual Accounts and Consolidated Annual Accounts Law. (The others reported they would either consider applying IFRS or that the costs of implementing IFRS would be overly prohibitive.) In a 31 March 2016 letter from Latvian Prime Minister Māris Kučinskis to the OECD Secretary-General, however, the Latvian government expressed a commitment to apply IFRS to 14 out of Latvia's 15 largest SOEs (see Table 3.1). In addition, the government committed to working with the Ministry of Finance to consider broadening the range of SOEs that could have the option to apply IFRS to individual annual reports, as well as working with SOEs to help build their capacity.

Latvian authorities and representatives from the Latvian accounting and auditing profession further report that there is no expectation that the government will move to require further application of IFRS, though the Ministry of Finance at the time of writing was considering undertaking research on what the consequences would be if efforts were made to align Latvian GAAP with IFRS. Authorities suggest that, for the time being, the application of Latvian GAAP remains entrenched for a number of reasons that go beyond the scope of this assessment, including a lack of capacity to understand and/or to apply IFRS. Accountants and auditors only receive limited education on IFRS as part of their professional training, and there is little IFRS expertise outside the largest international accounting firms operating in Latvia. In addition, many Latvian companies (99.7%) are small or medium-sized and may therefore find IFRS disclosure requirements overly burdensome. Finally, according to LASA – and probably in relation to the capacity issues mentioned above – the State Revenue Service is reluctant to move away from Latvian GAAP, which is required of Latvian companies when they file their corporate income tax returns.[18]

Table 3.1. **Application of IFRS by large SOEs (as per the PPCSCL size threshold)**

Line ministry	SOE	Required/ recommended to apply IFRS under current framework?	Applicable law/regulation	Applies IFRS? (as of 01.2016)	Commencement of voluntary application of IFRS under Annual Accounts and Consolidated Annual Accounts Law
Agriculture	Latvijas valsts meži (Latvia State Forests)	Yes[1]	Consolidated Annual Accounts Law	No	2016
Economy	Latvenergo	Yes	FIML[3]	Yes	2016
Finance	Augstsprieguma tīkls ("High Voltage Network")	No	None	No	2016
	Latvijas Loto (Latvian lottery)	No	None	No	No plan
	Valsts nekustamie īpašumi ("Country Real Estate")	No	None	No	Partially in 2016; fully in 2017
Health	Rīgas Austrumu klīniskā universitātes slimnīca (Riga Eastern Clinical University Hospital)	Yes[1]	Consolidated Annual Accounts Law	No	2016
	Paula Stradiņa Klīniskā Universitātes slimnīca (Pauls Stradins Clinical University Hospital)	Yes	None	No	
	Bērnu slimnīca (Children hospital)	Yes	None	No	
Transport	Ceļu satiksmes drošības direkcija (Road Safety Directorate)	Yes[1]	Consolidated Annual Accounts Law	No	2017
	Latvijas autoceļu uzturētāj (Latvian Road Maintenance)	No	None	No	2016
	Latvijas dzelzceļš (Latvian Railways)	Yes[1]	Consolidated Annual Accounts Law	No	2016
	Latvijas gaisa satiksme (Latvian Air Traffic)	No	None	Yes[2]	2016
	Latvijas Pasts (Latvian Post)	Yes[1]	Consolidated Annual Accounts Law	No	2016
	Starptautiskā lidosta "Rīga" (Riga International Airport)	No	None	Yes[2]	2016
	Pasažieru vilciens (Passenger Train)	Yes[1]	Consolidated Annual Accounts Law	No	2016

1. As noted above, SOEs subject to the Consolidated Annual Accounts Law have the option to prepare their consolidated annual accounts according to IFRS.
2. Latvijas gaisa satiksme and Starptautiskā lidosta "Rīga" – which are neither listed nor in a company group situation – voluntarily apply IFRS in addition to Latvian GAAP in the preparation of their financial accounts.
3. Latvenergo has issued bonds and, as a result, is subject to the FIML's rules on the application of IFRS.

Source: Information provided by the Latvian authorities as of April 2016.

Audit standards (Principle V.C)

Principle V.C recommends that an annual audit should be conducted by an independent, competent, and qualified auditor, in accordance with high-quality auditing standards, in order to provide an external and objective assurance to the board and shareholders that the financial statements fairly represent the financial position and performance of the company in all material respects.

Regarding external audit requirements, CL Art. 176 requires all companies to submit their annual accounts to an audit by an auditor, who is elected in the meeting of shareholders. Art. 91 of the Annual Accounts and Consolidated Annual Accounts Law further specifies the scope of companies subject to audit by a sworn external auditor under the CL to those that exceed two of the three following size criteria: (1) a balance sheet total of EUR 800 000), (2) a net turnover of EUR 1 600 000, and (3) an average of 50 employees in the accounting year. Art. 91 also includes an external audit requirement applicable to all SOEs and all parent companies (even those exempted from obligations to draw up consolidated financial statements and a consolidated management report).

These provisions are complemented by the Nasdaq Principles, of which Principle 11.3 recommends that listed companies grant auditors access to the information they require to conduct an effective audit (followed by all 29[19] listed companies, as of end-2014), and Principle 11.4 requires auditors to provide independent and objective auditing and consultation services and to offer a systematic approach to risk management and control processes (which 25 of 29 companies reported fully complying with; 3 reported partial implementation). Finally, pursuant to the Law on Sworn Auditors, sworn auditors and audit firms are required to undertake statutory audits in compliance with International Standards on Auditing (ISA) adopted by the International Federation of Accountants (IFAC).

Regarding measures to ensure auditors' independence, CL Article 176^{4} states that an auditor shall not be a shareholder, member of the management or supervisory board, or a person who is otherwise interested in the commercial activities of the company, or if the company is part of a group, may not be a shareholder or board member within a dependent or dominant company in the group. Auditor independence criteria are further elaborated under the Law on Sworn Auditors (Arts. 25-26).

Regarding measures to ensure the audit profession's conformity with professional standards and ethical norms, as well as other laws and regulations applicable to the audit profession, the Law on Sworn Auditors delegates certain supervisory tasks to the Latvian Association of Sworn Auditors (LASA), which is an independent professional corporation under the Ministry of Finance's supervision. (The Ministry of Finance develops and implements state policy in the field of auditing of commercial companies and is ultimately responsible for overseeing how LASA carries out delegated state tasks.) **LASA, whose** members include 169 sworn auditors and 140 licensed audit firms,[20] recognises the ISA and supervises the application of these standards in Latvia; this includes responsibility for quality control reviews of the sworn auditors and audit firms in disciplinary proceedings. Other LASA responsibilities established under Art. 6 of the Law on Sworn Auditors include: representing and defending the interests of LASA members, organising qualification examinations for sworn auditors, deciding on the issuance of a certificate to a sworn auditor and on the issues of a license to audit firms, organizing the Sworn Auditor Register and the Register of Commercial Companies of Sworn Auditors, reviewing disputes between sworn auditors and clients at the request of one of the parties to the dispute, organizing and supervising continuous education of sworn auditors, and performing other tasks as prescribed by the Law on Sworn Auditors and LASA's articles of association.

LASA may initiate disciplinary proceedings against a sworn auditor at the proposal of the court, the complaint of a legal or natural person, or on its own initiative, and it should inform the Ministry of Finance in writing, as per Art. 38^{1} of the Law on Sworn Auditors. (The number of sanctions applied by LASA through end-2014 is shown in

Table 3.2 below.) Under the Law on Sworn Auditors (Art. 40.2), the decisions taken by LASA to certify sworn auditors, license audit firms, and other tasks the Law on Sworn Auditors delegates to LASA, or to apply sanctions, may be disputed to the Ministry of Finance. The Ministry of Finance's decision may be appealed in court.

Table 3.2 Sanctions Applied by LASA for violations of audit standards

Sanction	2010	2011	2012	2013	2014
Certificates suspended	4	0	5	3	0
Warning	4	3	5	2	3
Remark	1	6	5	1	2

Source: Information provided by the Latvian authorities.

The decision to apply sanctions may be taken by LASA following the results of planned or extraordinary LASA peer reviews. The Ministry of Finance carries out independent inspections, during which it also evaluates LASA's peer review process. The Ministry of Finance does not have the right to impose sanctions against a statutory auditor or audit firm, as it is a State policy-making institution and not a law enforcement body. Therefore, LASA has been delegated the task of taking disciplinary measures. In its capacity the Ministry of Finance has been responsible since 2010 for **(1) preparing annual programmes of inspections, (2) ensuring annual inspections of all sworn auditors that audit financial institutions and listed companies and are subject to inspection once every three years, (3) staffing teams of inspectors (the Ministry of Finance currently has five), (4) carrying out regular and extraordinary inspections, (5) assessing the annual summary received from inspectors on the results of the inspections and recommendations performed by the inspectors, and (6) preparing appropriate final reports.**

The Ministry of Finance may carry out an extraordinary inspection in order to (1) determine the causes hindering the provision of audit services, in accordance with the International Standards on Auditing (ISA) recognised in Latvia; or (2) obtain information on the quality of audit services provided by a particular sworn auditor or a commercial company of sworn auditors. The Ministry of Finance may also dispute LASA decisions (which are associated with the LASA's peer review findings in the course of an inspection), in which case the Ministry of Finance and LASA normally try to settle the dispute between them without taking legal action. (The Ministry of Finance, for example, could sue LASA regarding unlawful activities for activities that do not comply with LASA's articles of association.)

The framework for ensuring the competence of the audit profession is currently under review, as Latvia considers means for implementing the EU Audit Directive[21] and for applying the new Audit Regulation.[22] The Directive and Regulation require implementing jurisdictions to designate a competent authority/authorities with independence from the profession to oversee the audit profession. The Ministry of Finance has established a working group to implement the EU Directive and to apply the requirements of the EU Regulation. The issue regarding the designation of a competent authority that will oversee the application of the EU Directive and EU Regulation was resolved between the government and LASA in early 2016.

Audit and disclosure standards for SOEs and aggregate reporting (Guidelines VI. B and C)

SOEs, as commercial enterprises, are subject to the same audit requirements as those for private companies, described above, except for the provision in the new Annual Accounts and Consolidated Annual Accounts Law, which entered into force in January 2016, that will allow SOEs to choose to apply IFRS to the preparation of their financial statements beginning with the year 2016. SOEs are also generally subject to the same minimum disclosure requirements as all private companies. Latvian authorities add that SOEs may be subject to disclosure requirements under the Law on Freedom of Information, which is meant to ensure public access to information that is under the control of State administrative institutions and local government institutions, and the Law on Remuneration of Officials and Employees of State and Local Government Authorities, which requires members of SOE supervisory boards and management boards, as public employees, to submit declarations on their remuneration under the Law on Prevention of Conflict of Interest in Activities of Public Officials. Donations made by SOEs must also be disclosed under the Law on Prevention of Squandering of the Financial Resources and Property of the State and Local Governments.

Disclosure of material financial and non-financial information

Guideline VI.A addresses more specifically standards for disclosing material financial and non-financial information, including areas of significant concern for the state as an owner and the general public. Specific areas of disclosure under Guideline VI.A are detailed below:

Company objectives and their fulfilment (Guideline VI.A.1): Under the Guidelines, SOEs should disclose a clear statement to the public of enterprise objectives and their fulfilment. In its 2014 assessment, the Working Party had been critical of practices (or lack thereof) for defining and disclosing SOEs' public policy objectives and their fulfilment. Addressing these concerns are PPCSCL provisions requiring the Coordination Institution, line ministries, and SOEs to disclose information on SOEs' financial and non-financial performance. These provisions include:

- Art. 29.1, which calls on the Coordination Institution (1) to provide public access to SOE financial information via an interactive website that provides public access to an SOE sector database and (2) to develop guidelines for SOEs on the public disclosure of performance reports;
- Art. 29.2, which requires each line ministry to include on its website specific financial and non-financial information on each SOE in its portfolio and the ministry's ownership stake in each enterprise; and
- Art. 58, which requires similar disclosures by each SOE and each subsidiary (if one exists) on its own website, or on the website of its line ministry if the SOE has no website.

Latvian authorities reported that, in August 2016, the Coordination Institution will launch a new SOE sector website allowing public access to a database of SOE performance indicators. Meanwhile a number of line ministries and SOEs have already published at least some of the information required by the PPCSCL on their websites. (See, for example, Table 3.3 in section 3.2 below.) All SOEs were required to publish such information as of March 2016; at the time of writing, this process was ongoing.

In addition to disclosure requirements under the PPCSCL, SOEs are subject to CL requirements for all enterprises to indicate their commercial goals and main types of activities (Art. 144.1.3 and 144.2.4, respectively), as well as to submit annual accounts on the fulfilment of business objectives (Art. 174). (See section 3.3 below for more on setting and monitoring SOEs' commercial and public policy objectives.)

Financial and operating results (Guideline VI.A.2): Guideline VI.A.2 recommends the disclosure of enterprise financial and operating results, including where relevant the costs and funding arrangements pertaining to public policy objectives. In relation to this recommendation, the Latvian authorities explain that the Annual Accounts and Consolidated Annual Accounts Law specifies for all commercial enterprises in Latvia the content of the annual accounts required under CL Art. 144, described above. Minimum requirements apply equally to private companies and commercially oriented SOEs. Under Art. 8.2 of the Annual Accounts and Consolidated Annual Accounts Law, annual accounts must include a financial report and a management report. As per Art. 55 of the Annual Accounts and Consolidated Annual Accounts Law, management reports submitted with a company's financial reports must include (1) financial results indicators; (2) reference to sums specified in the financial statements and additional explanations about them; and, (3) for companies of a certain size,[23] the main non-financial indicators characterising the company and the relevant industry, i.e. information on the impact of environmental protection requirements and information on employees (for instance, the applied employment policy, guarantees and support to employees) or other information. The management report must also provide information on plans for the further development of the company; research and development measures, if applicable; branches of the company and representations abroad; use of financial instruments; and, if necessary, the company's risk management goals and policy. All companies must submit a copy of their annual accounts and a certified auditor's report (if it exists) to the State Revenue Service,[24] which is then required to transfer these documents to the Enterprise Register. The Enterprise Register then makes these documents public (Arts. 97-98 of the Annual Accounts and Consolidated Annual Accounts Law).

Annotations to Guidelines VI.A.2 note that, "when SOEs are expected to fulfil specific public policy objectives, information on the costs of related activities, and how they are funded, should be disclosed". In a change from previous pre-PPCSCL practice, Latvian SOEs must now publish online information on the fulfilment of their commercial and non-commercial objectives (Art. 58). (See also section 3.3.) The newly established Coordination Institution is responsible for ensuring compliance with the PPCSCL's disclosure requirements for SOEs and their line ministries. (See also section 3.3)

Remuneration (Guideline VI.A.4): The remuneration for members of SOE supervisory boards (where they exist) and management board members has to date been rarely disclosed in SOEs' financial reports. Latvenergo is one of the few SOEs to disclose this information and, in line with annotations to Guideline VI.A, does so on an individual basis.[25] More generally, this information can be gleaned from mandatory income disclosures to the State Revenue Service by management board members, who are considered public officials under the Law on Prevention of Conflict of Interest in the Activities of Public Officials.[26] This information is available on the State Revenue Service website, www.vid.gov.lv.

Latvian authorities noted that SOE executive remuneration currently applied is "substantially lower" in comparison to similar roles in the private sector and that this contributes to SOEs' difficulty recruiting professional, competent experts. On 22

December 2015, a new regulation on board remuneration prepared by the Coordination Institution received Cabinet approval. Latvian authorities report that the regulation could close the gap between remuneration rates for SOE management and supervisory boards and those paid in the private sector.[27] Latvian authorities also reported in April 2016 that the CSCC had concluded a public procurement for research services on private sector remuneration rates for management board members in Latvia, Lithuania and Estonia. The results of the study were expected by mid-June 2016 and could be used to elaborate guidelines for establishing SOE remuneration policies. The results could also potentially be used for amendments to national legislative acts on the remuneration of SOE management and supervisory boards. (See Table 3.5 in section 3.3 below on all guidelines and regulations prepared by the new Coordination Institution.)

Board member qualifications, selection and independence (Guideline VI.A.5): Art. 31 of the PPCSCL mandates that nominations to SOE supervisory boards and management boards should be public, fair and professional, and that potential candidates should be selected during a public application procedure. On 1 December 2015, the Coordination Institution received Cabinet approval for a new regulation on procedures for the nomination and composition of SOE supervisory boards. The new regulation includes a requirement for the shareholder to publish information on the board nomination procedure, including the name of the SOE; a description of the nomination criteria; the nomination committee's composition, evaluation criteria and methods; and the number of evaluated candidates. The regulation allows for the shareholder or the supervisory board to reject the nomination committee's recommendations and, in such cases, the shareholder is obliged to publish an announcement on the re-opening of the nomination procedure. (See section 3.3 for more on SOE board nomination processes.)

SOEs are not required to disclose information on board diversity policies, roles on other company boards, and whether they are considered as independent by the SOE board.

Material foreseeable risk factors (Guideline VI.A.6): All companies, including SOEs, are subject to Art. 55 of the Annual Accounts and Consolidated Annual Accounts Law, pursuant to which a company's management report must provide material information on the development of the company, financial results, and significant risks and any unclear circumstances the company may face. Regarding material risk factors, specifically, the management report should include financial risk management goals and policies; the adopted risk management policy for each significant forecasted future deal for which a risk-limitation accounting system is applied; and an assessment of the company's overall exposure to market risk, credit risk, liquidity risk and cash-flow risk.

Financial assistance and commitments made on behalf of SOEs (Guideline VI.A.7): This Guideline recommends that SOEs disclose any financial assistance, including guarantees, received from the state and commitments made on behalf of the SOE, including contractual commitments and liabilities arising from public-private partnerships. According to Latvian authorities, SOEs must report the receipt of State subsidies as part of the annual reports made by line ministries to the Cabinet under the Law on Budget and Financial Management. Of note, a 2012 government policy planning document that critically assessed Latvia's pre-PPCSCL corporate governance framework for SOEs reported that most SOEs were not reporting financial assistance received.[28]

Issues relating to employees and other stakeholders (Guideline VI.A.9): As described in further detail below (section 3.5), there is no formal requirement for SOEs to report on stakeholder relations.

Independent external audit

Guideline VI.B recommends that SOEs' financial statements be subject to an independent external audit based on high-quality standards. The Guideline also specifies that specific state control procedures do not substitute for an independent external audit.

In Latvia, SOEs of a certain size are required to submit their annual accounts to an audit by a certified external auditor under the CL (Art. 176) and the Annual Accounts and Consolidated Annual Accounts Law (Art. 91). The shareholders of SOEs subject to external audit requirements are responsible for appointing an external auditor from Latvia's pool of 169 certified auditors. The selection of an external auditor is subject to public procurement procedures and certified auditors can participate in open tenders to audit an SOE's books. Auditors' activities and auditor independence are regulated by the Law on Sworn Auditors.

The State Audit Office may also conduct audits of SOEs, as per the State Audit Office Law. As of end-2015, the State Audit Office had undertaken 25 audits of state and local government-owned enterprises since 2007.[29] These audits are non-financial probity audits of SOEs' performance and compliance with laws and regulations and are undertaken on an *ad hoc* basis. In the course of an audit, the Office can make recommendations for the rectification of discovered deficiencies.[30] Recommendations are included in the State Audit Office's audit report, which is published on the Office website. In the finalisation of the audit report, the Office and the audited bodies agree on a timeframe for implementing the Office's recommendations. Following the audit, audited bodies report directly to the State Audit Office on progress made implementing recommendations. The State Audit Office continually monitors implementation of its recommendations and periodically informs the Public Expenditure and Audit Committee of the Parliament on progress made in this regard.

Finally, internal audit procedures for SOEs are not mandated by law. Some large SOEs have voluntarily introduced internal audit procedures.

Aggregate annual reporting on SOEs

Guideline VI.C recommends that government ownership entities develop consistent reporting on SOEs and publish annually an aggregate report on SOEs. The Latvian government published the last aggregate report on the SOE sector in 2009. The first annual aggregate report under the PPCSCL, as noted above (section 2.1), was published on 16 February 2016, covering the 2014 calendar year.[31] This first aggregate report, Latvian authorities explain, serves as a structural model for future reports. Latvian authorities report that it includes an aggregate evaluation of the State's overall SOE assets, divided by sector and an explanation of SOEs' non-commercial objectives, as identified by SOEs in 2014 (prior to the 1 January 2015 entry into force of the PPCSCL).

SOEs' reporting against their mid-term operations strategies and the Coordination Institution's assessment of these reports will provide the baseline content for future annual aggregate reports on Latvia's SOE sector. Latvian authorities explain that, for future reports, they expect line ministries to submit their evaluation of SOEs' performance assessments by June. Under the PPCSCL, the Coordination Institution then has until 30 August year to submit to the Cabinet and the Saeima the annual aggregate report for the previous calendar year (PPCSCL Art. 30).

Disclosure of governance, ownership and voting structures for publicly traded companies

Principle II.E.2 recommends requiring the disclosure of capital structures and control arrangements, and **Principle V.A.3** similarly recommends requiring the disclosure of material information on major share ownership, including beneficial owners, and voting rights.

Regarding the disclosure of control arrangements and share ownership, two laws generally apply: the FIML and the GCL, complemented by the Nasdaq Principles. Art. 56^1 requires listed companies to disclose information on control arrangements and share ownership in their annual reports/accounts. Required disclosures include capital structure, classes of shares and voting rights, major share ownership, and shareholder agreements (confidential for unlisted companies), among others. Art. 61 of the FIML stipulates that a person who directly or indirectly acquires (or disposes of) the shares of a listed company exceeding (or falling below) the thresholds of 5, 10, 15, 20, 25, 30, 50, and 75% of shares shall notify the Commission, as well as the listed company itself. The next steps for the listed company are to make this information publicly available on ORICGS, and then to make it available to third parties. The FIML also requires listed companies to include in their published annual report the list of the shareholders who own more than 5% of the voting shares at the end of the respective financial year.

Additionally, the Nasdaq Principles encourage listed companies to ensure that the investor relations section of the company's website contains information on the company's shareholders who own at least 5% of the company's shares, and to disclose information on changes in shareholders. The recommendation lists 12 separate sub-items regarding information to be disclosed in the investor relations section of the website – with which 23 of 29 listed companies reported full compliance.

For company groups subject to the GCL, shareholders are obliged to conform to additional rules regarding disclosure of information on share ownership. A shareholder who acquires more than 10% of the shares of such a company has a duty to notify the company in writing of the total number of his or her shares, as well as the voting rights associated with these shares. The GCL requires the shareholder to notify of any further increases or decreases of shares by increments of 5%, as well as if ownership decreases below the 10% threshold. A person who holds shares in his or her name but for the benefit of another person has a duty to indicate the beneficial owner of shares. A shareholder is obliged to notify the company within two weeks from the date of acquiring or disposing shares. The company has a duty to reflect this information in an annex to the annual accounts.

Regarding the more specific requirement to disclose information on beneficial owners, Art. 17^1 of the CL requires a shareholder to notify a company in writing within 14 days if he or she holds at least 25% of shares in a company for the benefit of another natural person. If the shareholder holds shares on behalf of a legal person, then the shareholder must indicate to the company, the founders or shareholders of the legal entity. Procedures for providing information to a company on beneficial ownership are provided in Art. 6 of the Group of Companies Law. The definition of beneficial owner applied in the CL is provided in Art. 1.5 (a-b) of Latvia's Law on the Prevention of Money Laundering and Terrorism Financing,[32] which defines a beneficial owner as a natural person:

a) who owns or directly or indirectly controls at least 25% of the merchant's fixed capital or the total amount of voting shares, or who controls the merchant's activity in any other way;

b) who directly or indirectly has the right to property or who directly or indirectly controls at least 25% of a legal entity other than a merchant. A person or a group of persons for whose benefit an establishment has been set up is considered the beneficial owner of the establishment. A political party, partnership or cooperative society is considered the beneficial owner of the relevant political party, partnership and cooperative society.

Art. 17^1 of the CL also requires a company to provide the beneficial ownership information provided by the shareholder to the Enterprise Register. This information is available only to law enforcement authorities and control authorities in the fields of tax administration, public procurement, and public-private partnership, and is mainly used for anti-money laundering purposes. The CL also requires that information on beneficial ownership must be accessible by law enforcement authorities and authorities in the field of tax administration, public procurement or also public-private partnerships.[33] FIML Art. 4^1.4 gives the FCMC the right to request this information from any person related to potential non-compliance with laws and regulations, or at whose disposal there is information that may be important in clarifying the circumstances of the breach.

Shareholders who fail to provide beneficial ownership information to a company, or who provide false information, are subject to criminal fines up to EUR 48 000 and/or a prison term of up to one year, under Art. 195^1 of the Criminal Law. Companies providing false information to the Enterprise Register are subject to criminal fines up to EUR 32 000, as per Section 272 of the Criminal Law. In addition, a company may be held liable under Latvia's corporate liability regime, provided under Art. 70^1 of the Criminal Law,[34] for criminal acts violating Arts. 195^1 and 272. Fines applicable under Art. 70^1 range from EUR 3 200 to EUR 32 million.

Regarding requirements to disclose information on company group structures, cross shareholdings, and intra-group relations, the AGM/EGM has an exclusive right to decide whether to enter into a group-of-companies agreement (a domination or profit transfer agreement). This decision may be taken if not less than three-quarters of shareholders with voting rights present vote for it, if the AoA do not require a larger proportion of votes. The group-of-companies agreement must be registered in the Register of Enterprises and it enters into effect only at the moment of registration.

Large and medium-sized companies are required to disclose this information under the Annual Accounts and Consolidated Annual Accounts Law (Art. 53.1.6), which requires companies to include in an annex a list of subsidiaries and associated companies, as well as the interest in their equity. The annex should also contain the amount of equity and the profit or loss of subsidiaries and associated companies. Similar information must be included in annexes to consolidated annual accounts prepared by parent companies of groups of companies. Companies in a contractual (and not *de facto*) group situation under the Group of Companies Law must also submit to the Enterprise Register the group's contract (including a description of the group's corporate structure), which the Register than publishes in the newspaper *Latvijas Vēstnesis* (Art. 13). Similar notification must be made to the Register when such a contract is terminated (Art. 17). Finally, Section 9 of the Nasdaq Principles requires listed companies to provide timely and exhaustive information on all substantial matters concerning the company, including its ownership structure, and to regularly verify, update and disseminate this information.

Regarding the disclosure of information related to voting rights, the CL permits companies to issue shares with different rights, but these are not commonly used in practice. The rights attached to various categories of shares may differ in respect to receiving dividends, receiving a liquidation quota or exercising the voting rights at the AGM/EGM. The information on categories of shares must be included in the AoA, the shareholder register and – in case of a new share issue – the regulations for increasing equity capital. The management board must ensure equal treatment of all shareholders that own shares of the same category.

SOE disclosure of governance, ownership and voting structures

Guideline VI.A.3 emphasizes the transparency of SOEs' *ownership and voting structures*, including legal ownership of the state's shares and any special shareholder rights or agreements. Regarding *disclosure of ownership*, Latvian authorities report that information on which ministries or agencies are responsible for exercising State ownership rights is publicly available, and information on corporate control structures is usually published on the respective SOEs' websites. (See Table 3.3 for examples of line ministries' websites.) SOEs in a group situation are also required to disclose ownership under the Group of Companies Law (Art. 6.1-3) and to disclose this information in the SOEs' annual accounts (Art. 8). Regarding *voting structures*, as noted above (section 2.1), the State does not have access to priority shares (i.e. "golden shares") and shareholder agreements are normally confidential in unlisted companies.

Table 3.3. **Line ministry websites disclosing state enterprise shareholding information**

Ministry	Website(s)
Ministry of Agriculture	• http://zm.gov.lv/zemkopibas-ministrija/statiskas-lapas/kapitalsabiedribas?nid=1224#jump
Ministry of Culture	• www.km.gov.lv/lv/ministrija/KM_institucijas.html
Ministry of Economics	• https://em.gov.lv/lv/par_ministriju/iestades__kapitalsabiedribas/informacija_par_kapitalsabiedribam/ • https://em.gov.lv/lv/par_ministriju/iestades__kapitalsabiedribas/kapitalsabiedribu_darbibas_rezultati/ • https://em.gov.lv/lv/par_ministriju/iestades__kapitalsabiedribas/pazinojumi_par_valdes_un_padomes_loceklu_nominesanu/
Ministry of Education and Science	• http://izm.gov.lv/lv/ministrija/struktura/kapitalsabiedribas
Ministry of Environmental Protection and Regional Development	• http://varam.gov.lv/lat/par_ministriju/padotas_institucijas/?info=3 • http://varam.gov.lv/lat/par_ministriju/padotas_institucijas/?info=16 • http://varam.gov.lv/lat/par_ministriju/padotas_institucijas/?info=23
Ministry of Finance	• http://fm.gov.lv/lv/finansu_ministrija/kapitalsabiedribas/
Ministry of Health	• www.vm.gov.lv/lv/ministrija/kapitalsabiedribas/
Ministry of Interior	• http://iem.gov.lv/lat/ministrija/valsts_kapitalsabiedriba_vsia_iekslietu_ministrijas_poliklinika/
Ministry of Justice	• https://www.tm.gov.lv/lv/ministrija/iestades
Ministry of Transportation	• http://sam.gov.lv/sm/content/?cat=477
Ministry of Welfare	• http://lm.gov.lv/text/72

Disclosure of related party transactions for publicly traded companies

Principle V.A.6 recommends requiring the disclosure of material information on related party transactions and the terms of such transactions to the market individually. Obligations to disclose related party transactions are included in the Annual Accounts and Consolidated Annual Accounts Law, the FIML, and under the Nasdaq Principles. (See section 3.1 above for the related assessment of Latvia's framework for supervision of related party transactions.)

However, as noted above, there is a risk that not all material related party transactions are disclosed under the current legal and regulatory framework. This is because the definition of "related party" is narrower under CL provisions guiding board review and approval of related party transactions than in the definition applied in the Annual Accounts and Consolidated Annual Accounts Law for the purpose of disclosing such transactions. (See Box 3.3 below for a summary of the legal framework for disclosing related party transactions.)

Also as noted above, the Latvian Ministry of Justice has undertaken a review of its framework for reviewing, approving, and disclosing related party transactions and established a working group to develop proposals for amendments to this framework, with a view to submitting draft legislative amendments to Parliament for review in September 2016.

SOE disclosure of material transactions with the state and other related entities (Guideline VI.A.8)

Regarding *transactions with the state*, as noted above (section 3.2, under "*Financial assistance and commitments made on behalf of SOEs*"), SOEs must report receipt of State subsidies as part of the annual reports made by line ministries to the Cabinet under the Law on Budget and Financial Management. Regarding *material transactions with related entities*, SOEs are subject to the same legal provisions regulating the review, approval, and disclosure of transactions with related parties. Prior to the entry into force of the PPCSCL, for SOEs without a supervisory board, state secretaries were individually responsible for reviewing and approving related party transactions.

Box 3.3. **Provisions for the disclosure of related party transactions**

Annual Accounts and Consolidated Annual Accounts Law (in force since 1 January 2016)

Article 53.1.14 requires the disclosure, in an annex to annual accounts, of information on transactions with related parties that have not been concluded under normal market conditions. This includes the amount of such transactions, the nature of the related party relationships and other information about the transactions necessary for an understanding of the financial position of the company (or the group of companies).

FIML

Article 57.4.2 requires listed companies that must prepare consolidated annual accounts to include in their interim management reports the following information about the most significant transactions with related persons:

- information about the transactions carried out with the related persons (undefined) during the reporting period where these transactions have had a significant effect on the financial standing or the financial performance of the capital company during that time; and
- information about any changes in the transactions with the related persons (undefined) that were disclosed in the previous annual report/accounts and could have a significant effect on the financial standing or the financial performance of the capital company during the reporting period. Where a capital company whose shares are admitted to trading on the regulated market does not draw up consolidated annual accounts, it shall disclose information about its transactions with the related persons in accordance with the requirements of the regulatory provisions of the home member state.

Article 59.2.23 defines as a significant event, which must be reported publicly, instances where an internal auditor's opinion identifies a transaction of significant volume between the issuer and a member of its management board or supervisory board or between the issuer and the related person of a member of its management board or supervisory board.

Group of Companies Law

While not limited strictly to related party transaction, Article 30 of the Group of Companies Law is relevant to this discussion. It requires dependent companies in a *de facto* group situation to submit annual dependency reports that include information on (1) transactions concluded by the dependent company during the accounting year with the dominant undertaking [i.e. company] with another undertaking that is merged with the dominant undertaking in a group of companies, as well as (2) the transactions concluded by the dependent company in the interests of such undertakings or as a result of an inducement, indicating in particular the transactions which are completely or partially disadvantageous to the dependent company or which involve a special risk for the dependent company or, also, which differ substantially from the entrepreneurial activities normally carried out. (On the basis of submitted consolidated annual accounts, Latvian authorities estimate that there are 300 company groups operating in *de facto* group situations to which Art. 30 would apply. Thirteen listed companies are considered to be the parent companies of *de facto* company groups.)

Nasdaq Riga Principles of Corporate Governance

Section 8.2 recommends each member of the management board to self-disclose to the board his or her conflict of interest (or the possibility of a conflict of interest) in any deal or agreement the company plans to conclude with a person to whom that member is related or connected. Section 8.2 imposes a parallel requirement on members of the supervisory board. In both provisions, a related party is defined as: "spouses, a relative, including kinship of second degree or brother-in-law of first degree, or persons with whom the board [or supervisory board] member has had a common household for at least one year." A connection with a board or supervisory board member is defined as: "legal persons where the board member or a closely related to him/her person is a [management board or supervisory board] member, performs the tasks of an auditor or holds another managing office in which he or she could determine or affect the business strategy of the respective legal entity."

Source: Information provided by the Latvian authorities as of April 2016 and texts of the laws cited here.

3.3. Establishing effective separation of the government's role as an owner of state-owned companies and the government's role as regulator, particularly with regard to market regulation.

The 2015 SOE Guidelines include a stronger focus on the overall responsibilities of the state ownership entity and, in assigning and implementing these responsibilities, ensuring that there is a clear separation between the government's role as an owner of state-owned companies and its role as regulator. This section assesses Latvia's position against relevant recommendations under the Guidelines in this regard, including the separation of functions (Guideline III.A), the state enterprise ownership policy (Guideline I.B), the SOE ownership rationale and SOE objective-setting (Guideline I.D), simplifying and standardizing SOE legal forms (Guideline II.A), SOEs' operational autonomy (Guideline II.B), the exercise of state ownership rights (Guideline II.D), and SOE board nomination processes (Guideline II.F.2).

Separation of functions (Guideline III.A)

Guideline III.A calls for a clear separation between the state's ownership function and other state functions that may influence the conditions for state-owned enterprises, particularly with regard to market regulation. As of end-2014, Latvian authorities stated there was no clear distinction, in practice, between the state's ownership function from other state functions that could influence conditions for Latvian SOEs, except perhaps in some specific instances (i.e. the provision of public utilities and enforcement of the Competition Law).[35] With the entry into force of the PPCSCL and adoption of amendments to the state enterprise ownership rationale in the SASL, however, there appears to be a recognition of the need to more clearly separate the state's functions vis-à-vis SOEs. (For a description of the PPCSCL and SASL see section 2.4.)

That said, Latvian authorities noted in the context of this review that, "of course, SOEs are considered as a vehicle for implementation of sectoral policies by sectoral policy departments [in SOE line ministries]." They added that, while line ministries' representatives (State Secretaries or Deputy State Secretaries) are never part of, or subordinate to, policy departments, they review and are responsible for the effective implementation of sectoral policies. In a number of cases, ministries are also the main or only shareholder in an SOE and its main or principal client; this is most often the case in relation to state-owned real estate enterprises.[36]

Ownership policy (Guideline I.B)

Guideline I.B[37] recommends the development of an ownership policy defining the overall rationale for state ownership. Latvia's rationale for state enterprise ownership is described in Art. 88 (1) of the SASL, which was amended on 22 October 2015 (see also section 2.4). Amendments to the SASL were developed as part of a broader SOE legislative reform package, submitted to Parliament in 2013, in part to address criticisms—from sources including the government itself – that Latvia's state enterprise ownership rationale may be interpreted too broadly. For example, the government's 2009 *Annual Review of Latvian State-Owned Assets* stated that "there is no clear policy to define which assets should be controlled by the State, municipalities, or other public sector authorities and why the State still owns many non-strategic assets without clear justification why the State should administer those assets."

The amended ownership rationale streamlines Latvia's ownership rationale by reducing the number of criteria from five to three: (1) to address cases of market failure and where "the market is incapable of ensuring protection of the public interests in respective area"; (2) to manage the delivery of services and goods "of strategic importance for the development of the administrative territory of the State or a local government or for national security"; and (3) to manage assets[38] that are of "strategic importance for the development of administrative territory of the State or a local government or for national security". These amendments, however, may not satisfactorily address concerns that the state enterprise ownership rationale could be interpreted too broadly. For example, the first criterion for justifying state enterprise ownership does not specify what steps would be considered to "ensure protection of the public interest". For the second and third criteria, the law does not specify what measure the government would apply for assessing when the delivery of goods or services or the management of certain properties would be "of strategic importance".

Latvian authorities explain that the Cabinet will determine how these terms are applied in practice. Guidance to this effect was developed by the Coordination Institution, underwent public consultation, and was approved by the Coordination Institution Council as of March 2016.

The authorities further explained that the adoption of the state enterprise ownership rationale triggers two provisions in the PPCSCL that could also clarify what the government considers to be measures for ensuring the "protection of the public interest" and what goods, services and properties are of "strategic importance". First, PPCSCL Art. 4 limits state enterprise ownership to conditions under which the criteria in Art. 88.1 of the SASL are met. Therefore, any decision to establish, maintain or increase state enterprise ownership under the PPCSCL must be aligned with the ownership rationale.

Second, Art. 25 requires line ministries wishing to either obtain or divest state shares in an SOE to submit a proposal to the Cabinet illustrating the conformity of the line ministry's decision with the ownership rationale. The same provision also requires each line ministry to assess its ownership portfolio according to the ownership rationale every five years. The first application of this provision was applied by line ministries in November 2015, when they were required to submit to Cabinet their proposals on ownership of SOEs in their portfolios. However, because line ministries' deadline for submitting their ownership proposals pre-dated the entry into force of amendments to the state enterprise ownership policy in the SASL, these proposals were assessed against the old version of the SASL. The outcomes of this exercise as of January 2016 are summarized in Table 3.4. The assessments draw upon a comprehensive assessment process carried out by the Cabinet of Ministers that resulted in a report accepted by the Cabinet in June 2013.[39]

Table 3.4. **Line ministries' enterprise ownership assessments under the PPCSCL, as of January 2016**

Line ministry	Ownership proposal	Line ministry's rationale for maintaining ownership	Cabinet assessment
Agriculture	To maintain state ownership in four SOEs: Latvijas valsts meži, Meliorprojekts, Zemkopības ministrijas nekustamie īpašumi, Latvijas Lauku konsultāciju un izglītības centrs	State ownership addresses a market deficiency and provides strategic goods and services as well as ensures management of strategic assets	Pending a redrafting of the ownership proposal in line with the new state enterprise ownership rationale in SASL Art. 88.1
Culture	To maintain state ownership in 16 SOEs and state shares in two enterprises where the State owns a minority of shares	State ownership addresses market deficiency (the private sector would not be interested in providing these services and fulfilling these societal interests) and ensures a higher quality of service/goods	Cabinet approval granted to maintain state ownership in 16 fully-owned SOEs and state shares in one minority-owned enterprise; Cabinet instructions to divest state shares in one minority-owned enterprise
Economics	To maintain state ownership of one SOE (the ministry will submit its proposals for other SOEs in the first half of 2016.)	State ownership addresses a market deficiency	Cabinet approval granted
Education	The ministry has not yet submitted proposals on any SOEs for which it is a shareholder	--	--
Environmental Protection & Regional Development	To maintain state ownership in three SOEs: Vides investīciju fonds, Latvijas Vides, ģeoloģijas un meteoroloģijas centrs, and Elektroniskie sakari	State ownership addresses a market deficiency, among other factors	Pending a redrafting of the ownership proposal according to the amended state enterprise ownership rationale in SASL Art. 88
Finance	To maintain state ownership in one SOE (Latvijas Proves birojs) (The Ministry will submit its proposals for other SOEs in the first half of 2016.)	State ownership addresses a market deficiency	Cabinet approval granted
Health	To maintain state ownership in all fully owned SOEs.	State ownership addresses a market deficiency. (The private sector would not be interested in providing these services and fulfilling these societal interests), safeguards a strategically important sector and ensures a higher quality of service/goods	Cabinet approval granted.
Interior	To maintain state ownership in one SOE (Lekšlietu ministrijas poliklīnika)	State ownership safeguards a strategically important sector.	Cabinet approval granted
Justice	To change the legal status of one SOE (Latvijas Vēstnesis) to a public agency from 2017 (the ministry will submit its proposal for another SOE, "Tiesu namu aģentūra", in the first half of 2016)		Cabinet approval granted
Transport	To maintain state ownership in all SOEs	State ownership addresses a market deficiency (the private sector would not be interested in providing these services and fulfilling these societal interests), safeguards a strategically important sector and ensures a higher quality of service/goods	Cabinet approval granted
Welfare	To divest state shares in five private enterprises owned by the State Social Insurance Agency (the ministry also submitted a proposal on one SOE on 9 February 2016)	For the one SOE: State ownership addresses a market deficiency	Cabinet approval granted

Source: Information as provided by the Latvian authorities as of January 2016.

SOE ownership rationale and objective-setting (Guideline I.D)

Guideline 1.D recommends that the state define the rationales for owning individual SOEs and subject these to recurrent review. It also recommends that any public policy objectives assigned to an individual SOE or group of SOEs should be clearly mandated and disclosed. As noted above in the discussion of disclosure of SOEs' public policy objectives (section 3.2), the Working Party had been critical of practices (or lack thereof) for defining and disclosing SOEs' public policy objectives and their fulfilment. As described in this section, the new PPCSCL introduces new requirements that could address these Working Party concerns.

Most Latvian SOEs have social and public policy objectives.[40,41] However, prior to the entry into force of the PPCSCL, there were no standard practices, laws, or regulations for balancing and disclosing commercial and non-commercial SOE objectives. Without a clear distinction of, and accounting for, commercial versus non-commercial objectives, it was difficult to assess whether an SOE was operating efficiently. Critics – including representatives of the Latvian government[42] – targeted unclear SOE objective-setting as one of the major obstacles to monitoring and assessing the sector's overall efficiency and transparency.[43]

Changes introduced by the PPCSCL could bring the objective-setting process for individual SOEs closer in line with the SOE Guidelines. First, at the State level, Art. 4 of the PPCSCL requires the ownership function to review its ownership rationale vis-a-vis individual SOEs. Under this provision, the State's ownership stake must (1) correspond with the overall state enterprise ownership rationale set forth in Art. 88.1 of the SASL and (2) help the SOE meet the objectives in its medium-term operation strategy. This evaluation must take place at least every five years, according to Art. 7 of the PPCSCL.[44] (This exercise has been applied once, to date; see Table 3.4 above.)

Second, at the level of SOEs, the PPCSCL requires each SOE to prepare a three-year medium-term operation strategy, which should include the elaboration of specific commercial and non-commercial objectives, as per Art. 57 of the PPCSCL. These strategies should also include an expression of the state's general strategic goal for state ownership in the SOE, as well as financial targets, capital structure objectives, and risk tolerance levels.

The first round of medium-term operations strategies was due from SOEs by March 2016. Since January 2016 the Coordination Institution has been responsible for assessing each SOE's medium-term operation strategy before it is assessed and approved by the line ministry. Although the Coordination Institution had expected to receive 42 strategies by end-March 2016, as of end-June 2016 only 13 strategies had been submitted. (At the time of writing, Latvian authorities report that a number of SOEs were in the process of developing new strategies or revaluating their current strategies to ensure compliance with the PPCSCL.) For each submitted strategy, the Coordination Institution has three months to review and provide feedback.[45] The Coordination Institution sees this task as a major test of its capacity and ability to work with line ministries. Once the medium-term strategies are approved, the Coordination Institution will also monitor the SOEs' implementation thereof, requiring the SOEs to submit regular assessments to the line ministries and to include this information in annual aggregate reports on the SOE sector.

Given that the Coordination Institution is newly established, it remains to be seen how these processes will be applied in practice, including the extent to which line ministries will heed the Coordination Institution's counsel regarding setting, balancing and monitoring implementation of individual SOEs' commercial and public policy objectives. In written responses to questions submitted to Latvia by the OECD Secretariat in preparation for this report in August 2015, Latvian authorities stated that the Coordination Institution "has no power to force shareholder[s] to heed [its] recommendations".

Simplifying and standardizing SOE legal forms (Guideline II.A)

Guideline II.A recommends that governments simplify and standardise the legal forms under which SOEs operate and that SOEs' operational practices follow commonly accepted corporate norms.

Latvian SOEs are normally established as either joint-stock companies or limited liability companies, though one statutory company was created in 2015: the aforementioned Altum, the development finance institution established under the Law on Financial Development Institution, which entered into force on 1 March 2015.) SOEs are not exempt from any laws and regulations that apply to private enterprises. This includes insolvency or bankruptcy to any special privileges or immunities.

With the adoption and entry into force of the PPCSCL, line ministries were required to submit to the Cabinet of Ministers and Coordination Institution by 1 November 2015 an assessment of their SOE portfolio and the rationale for maintaining state enterprise ownership of each SOE and for these entities' legal status. The Cabinet of Ministers, with input from the Coordination Institution, then decided on these proposals in January 2016. (See Table 3.4 above.) Such assessments of the State's ownership in each SOE should be undertaken every five years, as per the PPCSCL.

SOE operational autonomy (Guideline II.B)

Guideline II.B recommends that governments (1) allow SOEs full operational autonomy to achieve their defined objectives and (2) refrain from intervening in SOE management. The annotations clarify that governments may still act as active owners, but that direction given by the state to the SOE or its board should be limited to strategic issues and public policy objectives.

As a general rule, Latvian authorities assert that the government is not involved in the day-to-day management of SOEs and that SOEs are allowed full operational autonomy to achieve their defined objectives. As a general principle, under PPCSCL Art. 82 (applicable to state-owned LLCs) and Art. 118 (applicable to state-owned JSCs), SOE management boards are entitled to take decisions on all issues regarding the activity of a company, except those in which decisions in accordance with this Law and articles of association of the company are taken by the Cabinet, as well as the meeting of shareholders.

In practice, however, the Latvian authorities conceded that, under the pre-PPCSCL corporate governance framework, there was "significant political influence" over SOE governance and operational decisions.[46] This influence was facilitated by the lack of supervisory boards in most SOEs, which meant that the corporate management of SOEs was appointed and dismissed by the state secretaries of the relevant ministries. A specific example of a board function appropriated by state secretaries since the 2009 abolition of supervisory boards is the requirement that state secretaries personally approve all purchases above EUR 143 000. The pre-PPCSCL governance framework for Latvian

SOEs provided the State, and particularly state secretaries, considerable leeway to exercise direct influence if they so choose.

SOEs with non-government investors have enjoyed greater operational and management autonomy in the conduct of their commercial activities. This is the case, for example, at Air Baltic, which is 99.8% owned by the Ministry of Transport and 0.2% owned by two non-government shareholders, and at the formerly state-controlled Citadele, which until April 2015 was 75% owned by the Privatisation Agency and 25% owned by the European Bank for Reconstruction and Development (EBRD). Given that key provisions of the new PPCSCL have not yet been fully implemented, it may be too early to see how this practice will develop under the new SOE corporate governance framework.

Centralisation of the ownership function (Guideline II.D)

Guideline II.D recommends the exercise of state ownership rights should be clearly identified within the state administration and that the exercise of such rights should be centralised in a single ownership entity or carried out by a coordinating body. This "ownership entity", the Guideline further recommends, should have the capacity and the competencies to effectively carry out its duties.

As noted above, the PPCSCL created a new Coordination Institution, responsible to the Cabinet of Ministers. (See section 2.4 for an overview of the Coordination Institution and its tasks as provided in the PPCSCL.) On 12 May 2015, the Cabinet of Ministers appointed the Cross-Sectoral Coordination Centre (CSCC)[47] as the SOE sector's governance coordinating entity effective from 1 June 2015.

The Working Party has expressed concern that the Coordination Institution may not benefit from the financial and human resources necessary to fulfil its obligations under the PPCSCL. The Coordination Institution's resource requirements are not provided for in the PPCSCL, nor does it provide criteria for determining and meeting these needs. At the time of writing, baseline funding for the Coordination Institution's staff costs and operating expenses was included in the annual State budget for 2016 (EUR 268 000) and in the mid-term State budget for the years 2016-18. The funding covers the hiring of six personnel (of whom five had been hired as of January 2016) to work on SOE corporate governance, supervised by the deputy head of the CSCC. Latvian authorities admit this is a small team, stating that "the most crucial issue for the CSCC [operating as the Coordination Institution] is to ensure the necessary personnel for coordination of SOE governance." To this end, the CSCC reports that it will complement its resources with subject-matter expertise within line ministries[48] and within the CSCC's other teams, including the policy-making experts from the CSCC Development Planning Division.[49] Latvian authorities further stated that the Coordination Institution "has limited power to enforce directly some SOEs' governance regulations" but will be assisted in this regard by the new advisory Coordination Institution Council. Finally, the CSCC noted in April 2016 that, based on the experience of evaluating SOEs' medium-term operations strategies, it may consider requesting additional resources in the future, if needed.

Immediate tasks assigned to the Coordination Institution included preparing a number of guidelines and regulations required under the PPCSCL. (See Table 3.5 for a full list of pending guidelines and regulations.) As noted above, the Coordination Institution also sits on nomination committees for the nomination of SOE supervisory boards that can legally be re-established as of 1 January 2016 (see section 2.4 above and section 3.3 below); and will be reviewing SOEs' medium-term operations strategies (see section 3.3). These tasks will be among the first to test the Coordination Institution's capacity and line ministries' willingness to work with the Institution in a coordinated exercise of the state ownership function.

Table 3.5. **Status of guidelines and regulations prepared by the Coordination Institution as of end-June 2016**

Guidelines	Corresponding PPCSCL provisions	Status of completion as of end-June 2016
Guidelines for determining of general strategic aims of state participation	Art. 25.5	Approved by Coordination Institution Council
Guidelines for assessment of operation results of enterprise, in which the state has decisive influence	Art. 27.1	Approved by Coordination Institution Council
Guidelines for publishing of information for state owned enterprises and shareholders of state-owned enterprises	Art. 29.1.2	Approved by Coordination Institution Council
Guidelines on the order, in which institutions submit to the Coordination Institution information for preparation of the annual public report on enterprises and capital shares owned by the state	Art. 30.3	Approved by Coordination Institution Council
Guidelines for the preparation of medium-term operation strategy of an SOE	Art. 57.3	Approved by Coordination Institution Council
Regulations	**Correspondent PPCSCL provisions**	**Status of completion as of April 2016**
On order in which candidates are nominated for the positions of members of the management Board and supervisory boards in enterprises, where the state as shareholder (stockholder) has a right to nominate members of the management Board or the supervisory board, and members of the management Board in state enterprises where the supervisory Board is established	Art. 31.10	Approved
Standard articles of association for SOE (LLC and JSC)[1]	Art. 46.2	Approved
On criteria characterizing the size of company used to determine number of members of the management board and supervisory board members	Art. 79.1, Art. 106.3, Art. 114.1	Approved
On amount of compensation to institution responsible for sale of capital shares	Art. 143.3	Approved
Procedure of evaluation of operation and financial results of SOEs	Art. 27.7	Approved
Procedures on how decisions on prognosticated share of profit to be paid in dividends and share of profit to be paid in dividends are to made	Art. 28.6	Approved
Rules of procedures of Coordination Institution Council[1]	Art. 24.1-3	Approved
Rules on remuneration of the management board members and members of the supervisory board	Art. 79.4, Art. 112.1, Art. 117.1-2	Approved

1. Approved by the Cabinet as of October 2015.

Source: Information provided by Latvian authorities to the OECD Secretariat as of June 2016.

Board nomination processes (Guideline II.F.2)

Guideline II.F.2 recommends that the state, in exercising its rights as an informed and active owner, should establish well-structured, merit-based and transparent board nomination processes in full- or majority-owned SOEs and should actively participate in the nomination of all SOEs' boards and contribute to board diversity.

Under the PPCSCL, large SOEs[50] may have supervisory boards in place after 1 January 2016. According to the law, members are elected by the meeting of shareholders and elected to the Board for a five-year term (Art. 109). Candidates must have the appropriate professional and educational background to execute their duties as members of the board (Art. 108). The PPCSCL also lists the primary responsibilities of the supervisory board (Art. 107), which include overseeing the performance of the management board and its remuneration, approving operations strategies, and overall supervision of the SOE's business operations and reporting.

Nomination committees are responsible for nominating candidates for SOE supervisory boards, and line ministries with supervisory boards (where they exist) are jointly responsible for electing management board candidates. The process for nominating candidates under Art. 31 of the PPCSCL begins with, first, the shareholder – with assistance from the SOE supervisory board and from human resources experts – preparing a list of candidates. The shareholder then establishes a nomination committee to review the list of candidates. The nomination committee should consist of representatives nominated by the shareholder, the SOE supervisory board (if one exists), the Coordination Institution, independent experts and, if necessary, assessors with advisory rights. Finally, the nomination committee agrees on a candidate or a shortlist of candidates, which the shareholder or supervisory board can accept or reject.

The PPCSCL calls for the development of a government regulation further elaborating criteria for nominating SOE supervisory boards. This regulation was adopted by the Cabinet on 1 December 2015. The new nomination criteria regulation provides for the following:

- *Basic nomination criteria.* The regulation introduces more-detailed nomination criteria, including the compulsory requirement of tertiary education, knowledge of the Latvian language and at least one foreign language, appropriate work experience, and an unimpeachable reputation. The shareholder is allowed to define additional criteria, depending on the profile of the SOE.
- *Composition and role of the nomination committee.* The nomination committee must include representatives of the shareholder or supervisory board of the SOE, representatives of the Coordination Institution, independent experts and, if necessary, observers with advisory rights. Independent experts are natural persons who are not under the command of the shareholder or the supervisory board of the respective SOE. The nomination committee decides on evaluation procedures and can undertake its evaluation of candidates in several rounds. On the basis of these evaluations, the nomination committee recommends candidates for positions on the SOE management boards or supervisory boards.
- *Process for selecting and evaluating candidates.* The nomination process begins with the drafting of nomination criteria. After the criteria are approved, the shareholder should launch a public call for candidates; the use of international recruitment specialists is recommended. All information on candidates is strictly confidential and should not be transferred to any other persons. The shareholder and a board of directors have the right to reject recommendations of the nomination committee and to re-launch the nomination procedure; in this case, the decision to re-launch the procedure must be published publicly within three days of the decision.
- *Independence requirement.* At least half of supervisory board members should be independent directors. A director is considered to be independent if, (1) while working in another position, s/he is not under the command of the shareholder of

the respective SOE; (2) during the last three years, s/he was not a member of the management board or controller in the respective SOE or its subsidiaries; (3) s/he receives income from the SOE only as a member of the supervisory board; or (4) during the last three years, s/he was not an external auditor for the SOE or its shareholder, or a management board member or employee of the audit company that, during the last three years, has performed the function of external auditor for the SOE.

- *Transparency and disclosure.* As noted above (section 3.2), within three days of the nomination committee's decision to recommend a candidate or candidates, the shareholder must publish information on the nomination procedure, including the name of the SOE; a description of the nomination criteria; a description of the nomination committee's composition, evaluation criteria and methods; and the number of evaluated candidates.

3.4. Ensuring a level playing field in markets where state-owned enterprises and private sector companies compete in order to avoid market distortions.

This section focuses on recommendations in the SOE Guidelines for ensuring a level playing field and fair competition in the marketplace when SOEs undertake economic activities. This includes stakeholders' access to redress (Guideline III.B); transparency and disclosure of public policy objectives and their related costs (Guidelines III.C and D); the application to SOEs of general laws, tax codes and regulations (Guideline III.E); access to debt and equity finance (Guideline III.F); and SOEs' engagement in public procurement (Guideline III.G). (Guidelines Chapter III.A is addressed in section 3.3 above.)

Stakeholders' access to redress (Guideline III.B)

Guideline III.B recommends that SOEs' stakeholders and other interested parties, including creditors and competitors, should have access to efficient redress through unbiased legal or arbitration processes when they consider that their rights have been violated. In Latvia, SOEs may be challenged by stakeholders without restrictions. SOE stakeholders may enforce their rights through different mechanisms and a number of state institutions via civil action or administrative procedures. These include, for example, appeals for a direct compensation of damages due to a violation of law by an SOE, civil action for direct compensation for damages or other claims due to the violation by an SOE of a contractual obligation, and appeals on annulment of administrative or other acts issued by an SOE or state institution.

Transparency and disclosure of public policy objectives and related costs (Guidelines III.C & D)

Guidelines III.C and **III.D** recommend that state ownership entities and SOEs maintain transparency and disclose costs and revenue structures in cases where SOEs combine economic activities and public policy objectives. In the case of the latter, costs should be clearly identified, disclosed and adequately compensated by the state on the basis of specific legal provisions and/or through contractual mechanisms.

Before the entry into force of the PPCSCL, the only statutory obligation to communicate to the public on SOEs' objectives and their fulfilment was via annual reporting requirements under Art. 30^1 of the Law on Budget and Financial Management.

Under the PPCSCL, line ministries and SOEs – in cooperation with the Coordination Institution – must define their objectives and regularly disclose information on SOEs' financial and non-financial performance. (See sections 3.1 and 3.2 above for more on requirements to disclose public policy objectives and section 3.3 above for more on defining public policy objectives.)

Regarding the disclosure of costs and revenue structures related to public policy objectives, it is important to refer again, here, to the issue of the application of international accounting standards by at least large SOEs, as described in greater detail in section 3.2. As noted, SOEs' application of local accounting standards (Latvian GAAP) instead of IFRS could result in an unclear assessment of the true value of SOEs' assets and liabilities.

Application of general laws, tax codes and regulations (Guideline III.E)

Guideline III.E recommends SOEs undertaking economic activities should not be exempt from the application of general laws, tax codes and regulations, that laws and regulations should not unduly discriminate between SOEs and their market competitors, and that SOEs' legal form should allow creditors to press their claims to initiate insolvency procedures. Latvian authorities state that SOEs are not exempt from any laws and regulations that apply to private enterprises. This includes insolvency or bankruptcy procedures and is equally applicable to commercially and non-commercially oriented SOEs. (For example, Latvijas Pasts subsidiary Latvijas Pasta Nodaļu Tīkls was undergoing insolvency proceedings as of end-2014. Proceedings were initially launched in 2011.)

Access to debt and equity finance (Guideline III.F)

Guideline III.F recommends SOEs' economic activities should face market consistent conditions regarding access to debt and equity finance. In particular, the Guideline recommends: (1) SOEs' relations with all financial institutions, as well as non-financial SOEs, should be based on purely commercial grounds; (2) SOEs' economic activities should not benefit from any indirect financial support[51] that convers an advantage over private competitors; and (3) SOEs' economic activities should be required to earn rates of return that are, taking into account their operational conditions, consistent with those obtained by competing private enterprises.

SOEs' relations with financial institutions (Guideline III.F.1): State guarantees can only be issued within very limited cases, as stipulated under Art. 37(1) of the Law on Budget and Financial Management. According to this provision, State guarantees may be issued in support of State investment projects implemented by capital companies in which the state or local government owns at least 50%. The decision to provide the guarantee requires Cabinet approval, in accordance with the state annual budget law. If the Cabinet approves, the Ministry of Finance provides the guarantee.

Latvian authorities have highlighted the fact that there is no automatic guarantee in respect of SOEs' liabilities. Despite this assurance, however, the possibility cannot be discarded that perceived guarantees give some SOEs access to loans on preferential terms from commercial lenders. The fact that some SOEs are designated as "strategic" arguably sends a signal to markets that they most probably will not be allowed to fail. For example, Latvijas Dzelzceļš took out EUR 51 million in loans between 2007 and 2010 to finance construction projects, despite significant decreases in net profits and returns during the same period.[52]

Indirect financial support (Guideline III.F.2): SOEs are able to apply for State loans, as per Art. 36(5) of the Law on Budget and Financial Management, under which the Ministry of Finance and the Treasury can issue loans to SOEs where the State's fixed capital, separately or combined, exceed 50%. Latvian authorities informed the OECD Secretariat that such loans are rarely issued to SOEs, which instead generally raise capital on market terms from banks. Further, Latvia reports that SOEs do not receive preferential treatment by partially state-owned banks, as per Art. 4 of the Law on Prevention of Squandering of the Financial Resources and Property of a Public Person. This provision states that state-owned banks must grant loans in accordance with the procedures laid down in the Credit Institution Law and other laws and regulations.

SOE rates of return (Guideline III.F.3): As noted above (under Guidelines III.C and D), commercially oriented SOEs are generally not expected to generate profits but to meet costs.

SOE engagement in public procurement (Guideline III.G)

Guideline III.G recommends that, when SOEs engage in public procurement, procedures applied should be competitive, non-discriminatory and safeguarded by appropriate standards of transparency. Latvian authorities state that its Public Procurement Law applies equally to SOEs competing to win government public procurement contracts for a commercial activity. In these cases, SOEs must participate in the regular bidding process, alongside private sector competitors, and the State may not procure directly from an SOE. The Public Procurement Law does not apply, however, when the commissioning party enters into a contract regarding goods or services provided by institutions that are controlled or owned, directly or indirectly, by the commissioning party. These regulations appear to be in line with EU Public Procurement Directives and related case law in this area. A 2011 European Bank for Reconstruction and Development assessment of Latvia's public procurement framework came to a similar conclusion.[53]

3.5. Recognising stakeholder rights as established by law or through mutual agreements and the duties, rights and responsibilities of corporate supervisory boards.

This Roadmap core principle relates mainly to Chapters IV and VI of the Principles and Chapters V and VII of the Guidelines on stakeholders and boards. A full assessment of these chapters could potentially call for quite detailed information about actual board practices (including in relation to stakeholders). Therefore, this section focuses on some of the key framework conditions, including the legal framework defining the duties of board members, and the enforcement mechanisms and the legal rights of stakeholders. Specifically, it looks at Latvia's framework and practices regarding: (1) stakeholder rights (Principles IV.A, B and E); (2) the rights, duties and responsibilities of supervisory boards (Principle VI.A); and (3) SOE recognition of stakeholder rights and SOE supervisory boards (Guidelines V.A, B, C, and VII.C). Considering that the initial review of Latvia against the Principles identified Latvia's framework for insolvency as a key area of concern subject to a number of recent Latvian legal reforms and court activity, Principle IV.F calling for an effective and efficient insolvency framework and effective enforcement of creditor rights is also reviewed under this chapter.

Stakeholder rights

Respect for stakeholder rights (Principle IV.A)

Principle IV.A recommends that the rights of stakeholders that are established by law or through mutual agreements should be respected. Under Latvian law, the rights of stakeholders are generally protected. Latvia's self-evaluation reported that the legal rights of stakeholders are established by the Latvian Constitution,[54] in particular Chapter VIII, which outlines fundamental human rights for all Latvian citizens. Stakeholder rights are also protected in specific laws, including the Consumer Rights Protection Law (which protects consumers' rights when entering into contracts with manufacturers, traders or service providers), the Labour Law (regulating employment legal relationships), the Environmental Protection Law and the Law on Environmental Impact Assessment (regulating business' impact on the environment), and the Insolvency Law (which protects creditors' rights).

Latvia's legislation provides for remedial mechanisms for those stakeholders whose rights have been infringed. This is mainly achieved through Civil Law provisions establishing the use of pledge rights, guarantees or contracts to reinforce stakeholder rights, and through court proceedings that can be used to seek remedial actions or damages for a range of reasons. No information was available on the extent to which these mechanisms have been employed by stakeholders in practice.

Latvia has also adhered since 2004 to the OECD Declaration and Decisions on International Investment and Multinational Enterprises.[55] The OECD Guidelines for Multinational Enterprises have relevant recommendations to companies including on respect for labour rights and consumer protection.[56] To implement the Guidelines for Multinational Enterprises, Latvia has established a National Contact Point (NCP) and NCP Consultative Board, which comprises all relevant ministries and stakeholder organisations. The NCP provides for a grievance mechanism that may be used in cases in which the Guidelines for Multinational Enterprises are not followed, but so far this has not been used. The Ministry of Foreign Affairs provides the Secretariat for the NCP Consultative Board and also provides dedicated NCP pages on the ministry's website.

Finally, Latvia's self-evaluation reported that the respect for mutual agreements is protected under Art. 1587 of the Civil Law, which states:

A contract legally entered into shall impose on a contracting party a duty to perform that which was promised, and neither the exceptional difficulty of the transaction, nor difficulties in performance arising later, shall give the right to one party to withdraw from the contract, even if the other party is compensated for losses.

While the framework for establishing stakeholder rights appears in place, in practice, Latvia does not have a strong tradition of formal mechanisms to ensure the participation of employees and other stakeholders in corporate governance processes, such as employee participation on boards. Concerns have also been expressed about the effectiveness of protections for whistle-blowers: this is discussed in greater detail under IV. 4.5.1.3 (Principle IV.E) below.

Stakeholders' access to redress (Principle IV.B)

Principle IV.B recommends that, where stakeholder interests are protected by law, stakeholders should have the opportunity to obtain effective redress for violation of their rights. In Latvia, stakeholders are entitled to seek redress through the courts. However, since the financial crisis and the ensuing spike in insolvency cases heard by Latvian courts, it can take many months – and sometimes years – to resolve a civil or commercial dispute in court, resulting in a high backlog of cases. Going to court may also be cost-prohibitive for some stakeholders, while few have confidence in Latvia's unwieldy arbitration system. This could improve under the new Mediation Law and the new Arbitration Law (see section 2.2 above). Also as noted above, Latvia has taken steps to address the shortcomings of its court system.

Latvia's self-evaluation also reported that stakeholder protections are monitored via specialized bodies, including the Consumer Rights Protection Centre, protecting rights enshrined under the Consumer Rights Protection Law; the State Labour Inspectorate, which monitors legal employment relationships, occupational safety and health issues; and the State Environmental Service, which monitors implementation and enforcement of Latvia's environmental protection laws.

Communicating concerns about illegal or unethical practices (Principle IV.E)

Principle IV.E recommends that stakeholders, including individual employees and their representative bodies, be able to freely communicate their concerns about illegal or unethical practices to the board and to the competent public authorities and their rights should not be compromised for doing this. As of end-2014, there was no standalone whistle-blowing law in Latvia for reporting illegal or unethical practices to the supervisory or management board and for protecting those who report such practices in good faith. All Latvian citizens have the right to submit complaints in written form to institutions responsible for implementing State administration tasks under the Law on Submissions. Under this law, the responsible government body must reply within one month (Art. 5.3), but the law does not require that the complaint be resolved. Other relevant laws include the Law on Special Protection of Persons (which only applies to witnesses in criminal proceedings), and the Law on Prevention of Conflict of Interests in Activities of Public Officials (for public officials reporting conflicts of interest).[57] The Latvian authorities further explain that whistle-blowers are protected from retaliation – depending on the circumstances of the case – under the Labour Law and the Criminal Law. Under the Labour Law, the onus is on the employer to prove that the employee has not been punished or faced adverse consequences, either directly or indirectly, as a result of reporting illegal or unethical practices.[58] Nevertheless, Freedom House, an NGO that reviews countries' levels of democracy, expressed concerns about inadequate protection for whistle-blowers in its most recent report.[59]

Latvian authorities concede that there is no comprehensive legal framework to protect whistle-blowers.[60] As a result, a working group led by the State Chancellery had at the time of writing prepared a draft law regulating protections for both public and private sector whistle-blowers and procedures for whistle-blowing, which is foreseen to be monitored by the Corruption Prevention and Combating Bureau (KNAB). The government reported that, as of April 2016, it planned to seek approval of the law in 2016 to enter into force in January 2017.

Insolvency framework and enforcement of creditor rights (Principle IV.F)

The 2014 review of Latvia against the Principles identified the effectiveness of the framework for insolvency as an important concern that would require further attention as part of a broader effort to deepen Latvia's capital markets and to increase investment in the country's private sector. Thus, this report focuses more specifically on Latvia's implementation of **Principle IV.F,** which states that the corporate governance framework should be complemented by an effective, efficient insolvency framework and by effective enforcement of creditor rights.

A revised Latvia Insolvency Law came into force in 2010. The law was developed with technical assistance from the IMF as part of overall structural reforms Latvia enacted in compliance with the terms of its financial assistance agreement with the Fund. The law facilitates the settlement of situations between a viable performer of economic activity and its creditors, and aims to ensure effective legal protection proceedings and creditor rights. It also provides for personal bankruptcy procedures. The law, according to the IMF and the World Bank, is in line with internationally accepted insolvency standards, including the UN Commission on International Trade Law (UNCITRAL). As a result, Latvia's self-evaluation reported that insolvency proceedings have become simpler, faster and more effective. This assessment is supported by Latvia's improved rankings in the World Bank's 2014 *Doing Business* report[61] for resolving insolvency cases (improving from 46th in 2013 to 43rd in 2014) and the *EU 2015 Justice Scoreboard*, which noted the improvement in insolvency case clearance rates between 2010 and 2013.[62] (These improvements may be due in part to the slowdown in insolvency cases in the years following the financial crisis, when Latvian courts were flooded with insolvency-related cases.[63] See Table 3.6, which includes data reported by the government on the number of insolvency proceedings following Latvia's economic downturn of 2008-09.)

Despite the progress in recent years to improve insolvency case clearance rates, the effectiveness of Latvia's insolvency framework in practice has been the subject of much attention and criticism from a variety of sources, both domestically and internationally, due in part to the still-significant backlog of cases that accrued following Latvia's economic downturn of 2008-09 and allegations of abuse by insolvency administrators.

The backlog of insolvency cases has resulted in significant economic costs for Latvia. An independent study undertaken on FICIL's behalf[64] of 9,512 companies that were announced insolvent between 2008 and 2014 estimates that total economic losses due to unrecovered creditor claims and costs related to insolvency proceedings during this period totalled EUR 6.9 billion, including EUR 0.5 billion lost due to insolvency abuse. The study also shows that (1) the average recovery rate of secured creditors in Latvia was 42% over the last three years, which is substantially below the average recovery rate for secured creditors in OECD high-income countries (72%), and (2) the recovery rate of unsecured creditors (including the State Revenue Service) in the last seven years was less than 1%.

Table 3.6 Insolvency case statistics

	Natural persons		Legal persons	
Year	Announced insolvency proceedings	Completed insolvency proceedings	Announced insolvency proceedings	Completed insolvency proceedings
2014	1 289	381	960	389
2013	1 571	58	820	629
2012	1 375	7	881	880
2011	849	1	879	1 166
2010	199	0	2 574	1 151
2009	53	0	2 149	900
2008	1	0	1 289	225

Source: Latvian responses to follow-up questions from the Secretariat, received 18 August 2014.

A number of observers have, as noted, criticized Latvia's insolvency framework as prone to abuse. An IMF report (IMF, 2013) states that, in 2011, there were reports that a number of financially sound companies nevertheless were subject to insolvency proceedings. In addition, a Council of the European Union (2013) expressed a range of concerns about the functioning of the civil justice system, including the reliability of insolvency administrators. Finally, the abovementioned September 2015 FICIL position paper concludes that "the absence of the government's insolvency policy [and] chaotic and fragmented monitoring process of insolvency proceedings, as well as [the] ineffectiveness of law enforcement bodies[,] is the main reason for low inefficiency rates of [the] insolvency system". It recommends that the government draft a long-term insolvency policy, establish a transparent supervision and monitoring system, and fight those who abuse the law.

These criticisms were shared by Latvia's State Audit Office, which in March 2015 issued a critical performance audit report[65] on the functioning of the insolvency framework. The report criticized the government for adopting legal reforms in 2010 "in haste" based on advice from the IMF, without properly taking account of local conditions. As a result, the report states, Latvia relies on insolvency administrators that are not sufficiently monitored by an oversight body, and under which creditors who have a vested interest in the outcome practically play the role of overseeing administrators. With much of the priority in the reforms given to improving the speed with which insolvency cases are resolved (due to the large backlog of cases developed in the wake of the financial crisis), there has not been sufficient focus on the conservation and recovery of economic value, reflected in the low recovery rates of creditors' funds – just 14% of claimed amounts. The report further criticizes the Ministry of Justice for not developing a strategy, objectives and quantifiable indicators to monitor and improve the functioning of the system over time.

Considering the above criticisms and the large number of cases – including a high-profile pending insolvency case involving one of Latvia's largest listed companies, the steel manufacturer Liepajas Metalurgs (see Box 3.4) – the Latvian government has responded by taking a number of steps to improve the efficiency of the judicial system, including hearing insolvency cases (see section 2.2), strengthening ADR mechanisms, and proposing amendments to the Insolvency Law.

Box 3.4. **Insolvency framework in practice: Liepajas Metalurgs**

In 2013, Latvia's largest steelmaker, Liepajas Metalurgs (LM), was declared insolvent. The LM insolvency proceedings, which were ongoing at the time of writing, provide an illustration of the application of the 2010 Insolvency Law in practice.

Prior to its insolvency, LM was one of Latvia's largest listed companies. According to IMF estimates, LM's net turnover equalled about 2% of GDP and 4.4% of exports in 2012, and the company employed some 2,300 workers, or 0.3% of Latvia's national labour force. In July 2013, after several quarters of poor performance, the government assumed liability for a EUR 67 million loan from Italy's UniCredit Group to LM that the Treasury had guaranteed in 2009 to support LM's expansion, after already paying back a EUR 6.2 million principal instalment for the state-guaranteed loan. LM was listed on the Nasdaq OMX Baltic Secondary List until it was delisted on 27 December 2013, due to LM's becoming insolvent.

In the period leading up to LM's eventual default on the loan, there has been ongoing coverage in the Latvian media of criminal investigations involving two of LM's largest shareholders, and conflicts of interest involving the auditor of LM's financial reports. Sergejs Zaharins and Ilja Segals, who reported ownership of 49% and 21% of the company, respectively, were publicly designated as suspects in a criminal investigation related to alleged personal benefit from corporate funds in the summer of 2013, and a third shareholder (with 23% ownership) and former vice-president of the company, Kirovs Lipmans, was identified as a victim in the case. However, this status was cancelled by court decision in January 2014 due to insufficient evidence.

In addition, the State Audit Office raised concerns about the accuracy of Liepajas Metalurgs' annual financial reports on which the state guarantee was based in September 2013, pointing out that one of LM's supervisory board members, Andris Denins, was also a founder and board member of LM's audit firm, AS BDO. A subsequent review by the LASA concluded that the conflict of interest existed and that BDO should not have undertaken the statutory audit of LM. As a result, the auditor-in-charge, Mr. Aivars Putnins, had his state auditor's certificate suspended for one year in March 2014, a second BDO auditor was reprimanded and a third received a warning. All three disciplinary actions were disputed to the LASA Board. One disciplinary action – a warning – was cancelled. One disciplinary action – suspension of validity of the certificate – was disputed to the Ministry of Finance. The Ministry of Finance decided to leave the decision of the LASA unchanged. The LASA also found significant deficiencies in the 2012 audit of LM, triggering an obligation for LASA to undertake future follow-up quality reviews.

In November 2013, the Liepaja Court launched an insolvency process after LM's insolvency administrator, Mr. Haralds Velmers, submitted an insolvency application to the court. Following the launch of the insolvency process, LM was placed under the supervision of Mr. Velmers, who would be responsible for overseeing the sale of LM within six months of the Liepaja court's ruling on LM's insolvency, as per the sale schedule set forth in Art. 111 of the Insolvency Law.

In March 2014, the Latvian firm Prudentia was chosen by LM's insolvency administrator to oversee the sale of LM's assets via an international tender and/or auction. LM's secured creditors – "Citadele banka", "SEB banka", and the State Treasury – were consulted on, and agreed to, the LM sales plan. According to the IMF, a sale in which LM's assets could remain whole would be preferable, as these assets would be more valuable when taken together, maximizing the recovery value and facilitating LM's reopening.

Box 3.4. **Insolvency Framework in Practice: Liepajas Metalurgs** (cont.)

In June 2014, Mr. Velmers announced that the total approved sum of creditor claims was EUR 200.2 million, involving EUR 114.8 million claimed by secured creditors and EUR 85.3 million from unsecured creditors. On 28 August 2014, it was decided to extend the term for the sale of assets for an additional six months, until 27 February 2015. Prudentia announced plans to sign a letter of intent for the sale of the main assets of LM's production facility on 9 September, indicating that a Ukrainian company, the KVV Group, had offered EUR 107 million. No further information was available at the time of writing on the potential value of remaining assets or on the likelihood that the insolvency process will lead to a full recovery of creditors' claims. The terms for selling LM's property have been delayed one more time since February 2015, on 27 August 2015. The plan at the time of writing was to sell all of LM's assets by 26 February 2016.

Sources : Information provided by Latvian authorities through October 2015; FinanceNet, *http://financenet.tvnet.lv/zinas/480673-aptur_darbibu_liepajas_metalurga_revidentam_auditorfirmai_bdo;* *Baltic Times*, "Liepajas Metalurgs starts insolvency", 13 November 2013 (*www.baltictimes.com/news/articles/33745/#.U7vUrvmSx1Y*); IMF (2014), *Republic of Latvia: 2014 Article IV Consultation—Staff Report; Press Release; and Statement by the Executive Director for the Republic of Latvia*, IMF, Washington DC (*https://www.imf.org/external/pubs/ft/scr/2014/cr14115.pdf*); Liepajas Metalurgs announcement of the sale of LM steel mill assets, *http://lm.metalurgs.lv/important/LM_advertisment_en.pdf*; Nasdaq GlobeNewswire, "AS "Liepājas metalurgs" to be delisted from the Baltic Secondary list", 20 December 2013 (*http://globenewswire.com/news-release/2013/12/20/598718/0/en/AS-Liep%C4%81jas-metalurgs-to-be-delisted-from-the-Baltic-Secondary-list.html#sthash.WGdHaGkI.dpuf*); Prudentia, "LETA: Sales process of insolvent JSC "Liepājas Metalurgs" will be organized by Prudentia", 21 March 2014 (*http://prudentia.lv/public/33773.html*), and various media reports in Latvian and Russian-language press.

Amendments to the Insolvency Law were adopted in the Parliament's third reading on 25 September 2014 and took effect on 1 March 2015. These amendments provide clarifications and adjustments to frameworks and conditions under which insolvency proceedings may be declared for both legal persons (generally referring to enterprises) and natural persons (i.e. personal bankruptcy, which generally involves smaller amounts and may include families, or founders or shareholders of a fisherman's or farm household).

The amendments to Latvia's insolvency framework that have attracted the most attention have been the designation of insolvency administrators as public officials and the stipulation that insolvency administrators must follow the same legal requirements as public officials related to reporting on conflicts of interest and income. The Latvian Association of Certified Administrators of Insolvency Proceedings, many of whose members also work as lawyers, has challenged these provisions in court, saying that it would impose unconstitutional restrictions on its members' ability to make a living by restricting their ability to work as lawyers at the same time that they are serving as insolvency administrators. The Latvian authorities have asserted that new restrictions and requirements for the insolvency profession – including provisions for training and certification, as well as penalties for violations – have become necessary, due to the high number of complaints received about insolvency administrators' actions (an average of more than 300 complaints filed annually – nearly 15% of the number of cases that have been filed each year).[66] At the time of writing, the Constitutional court had postponed implementation of the provisions relating to the insolvency profession until spring 2016, while the Court reviews these provisions.

In June 2015 the Ministry of Justice also established a Working Group on Insolvency[67] that is being used to collect input to the government's future strategy for overseeing the insolvency framework. The Ministry's aim is to have insolvency policy goals through 2020 developed by the end of 2016. The Ministry has also obtained further technical assistance from the IMF to develop a pilot project to monitor the effectiveness and efficiency of the system through indicators dealing with such issues as rates of recovery, costs and speed of resolution. Parliamentary discussions of possible further reforms on the status of insolvency administrators are expected to resume once the Constitutional Court has issued a decision on its review of the challenge to the current law.

The rights, duties and responsibilities of supervisory boards

Principle VI.A recommends that board members should act on a fully informed basis, in good faith, with due diligence and care and in the best interests of the company and its shareholders.

CL Art. 169 states that members of the management board and supervisory board shall be "solidarily" (i.e. jointly) held liable for losses they have caused the company. However, if the management board members or directors can prove they acted as an "honest and careful manager," then they are not considered liable for losses caused to the company. Nor shall they be liable, under Article 169(4), "if he or she has acted in good faith within the framework of a lawful decision of the meeting of shareholders."

One question FICIL raised during the OECD Secretariat's fact-finding visit to Riga in mid-2014 was its interest in seeking clarification of how the term "honest and careful manager" should be interpreted in this context in order for board members to escape liability for losses that their decisions may cause to the company. The Ministry of Justice provided summaries of 14 cases through 2014 of the Cassation instance of the Supreme Court that have further interpreted these provisions.[68] For example, one case decided on 15 January 2014 involved a company that brought a claim against a former management board member for withdrawing money from the company's account without legal justification. The Court found that the company had no obligation to prove the liability of the management board member, which was presumed. Rather, the burden of proof was on the management board member to prove that he or she acted as a careful manager. The legal reasoning of the decision further specified that the management board member is obliged to act in the best interests of the company and perform their duties with the greatest care (due diligence) and on a fully informed basis, and must put the interests of the company first. A second judgement of the court on 27 May 2014 made reference to a 2012 judgement stating that "honest and careful manager" is a term with "general content", and that the duty of the court is to make further interpretation of the term in order to achieve an equitable solution to the dispute.

In their totality, if properly enforced, the courts' interpretation of CL provisions related to board liability would appear to underpin both a duty of loyalty and a duty of care to act in the best interest of the company and its shareholders. While a number of the cases related to management board liability, one could extend the application of these interpretations to liability for members of supervisory boards. The law itself is less explicit with respect to the board's duty to shareholders than to the company, but it does include provisions to ensure that shareholders have the right to make claims against board members for not acting in the best interests of the company, as described further below. Moreover, the concept of a board member's duty to shareholders is recognized under Nasdaq Principle 6, which states that the objective of the board "is to act in the interests of all the shareholders, ensuring that the value of the Issuer grows."

One aspect of board liability that could lead to some confusion in the Latvian framework is in the case of controlled companies within company groups operating under Latvia's Group of Companies Law. The management board members of such companies may be bound by contractual agreements that give the controlling company the right to give instructions to the management board of a controlled company – even in cases that may cause damages to the controlled company if they conform to the interests of the group of companies. Although the management board of the controlled company has a duty to implement the instructions issued by the controlling company, the management board of the controlled company still owes its duties only to the controlled company, leaving some legal uncertainty as to how these duties should be resolved when they come into conflict. The Latvian authorities reported that no jurisprudence or regulations exist to clarify board member liability in relation to their duty to implement instructions by the controlling company.

Members of the management board and supervisory board may be held liable for damages caused to the company under CL Art. 172. This provision sets forth criteria for bringing an action against the founders, members of the management board or supervisory board, or the auditor on the basis of a decision taken during a meeting of shareholders by a simple majority of votes of those present. The company also has a duty to take an action against board members if requested by minority shareholders who represent at least 1/20th of equity capital or at least EUR 71 000 in equity. If the company does not take action within a certain time period, the minority shareholder also has the right to directly take action in the interests of the company. Judgements related to Art. 172 make clear that the board members' liability is to the company and not to individual shareholders. However, other judgments have further clarified that a board does not have the authority to stop an action against board members on behalf of the company without the consent of the minority shareholders who initiated the action.

Art. 173 of the CL outlines specific cases in which shareholders have the right to release members of the management board or supervisory board from liability. Under this provision, an individual may be exculpated from liability, or may enter into a settlement with the company, for an action he or she has taken that has caused the company losses. However, this does not restrict the rights of minority shareholders to seek action from the company or to bring an action directly against the board members for losses caused to the company, as per Art. 172(2) of the CL.

Representatives from listed companies' supervisory boards and management boards indicated that they do not consider being found liable for damages under Articles 169 and 172 as a major risk. They suggested that liability insurance for board members is more common in the financial sector, whereas few executives in non-financial listed companies feel the need to take out liability insurance.

Nevertheless, the summaries of cases provided by the Latvian authorities do show a number of cases providing recognition of minority shareholder rights and successful enforcement of the liability of board members through private actions. Furthermore, the Latvian authorities did not identify any cases in which the meeting of shareholders waived management board member liability. Data provided by the Latvian authorities indicate a substantial number of private enforcement cases, with nearly 1 000 decisions taken at the levels of first instance, appellate court and cassation court (Supreme Court level) related to board member liability under Articles 169 and 172. According to the Latvian authorities, most of these cases involved non-listed companies, but a more precise breakdown of the data was not available.

SOE recognition of stakeholder rights and SOE supervisory boards

This section assesses Latvia's position against Guideline V.A (recognising and respecting stakeholders' rights), Guideline V.B (reporting on stakeholder relations), Guideline V.C (internal controls, ethics and compliance programmes or measures) and Guideline VII.C (board composition and exercise of objective and independent judgment).

Recognition of and respect for stakeholder rights (Guideline V.A)

Guideline V.A calls on governments, the state ownership entities, and SOEs themselves to recognise and respect stakeholders' rights established by law or through mutual agreements. Stakeholders are accorded the same legal rights as those that apply to private companies, and no specific rights are granted to SOE stakeholders. The rights of stakeholders are generally protected under Latvian law, which, as assessed by the World Bank in 2002, generally reflect EU practices.[69] These legal rights are established in the Constitution of Latvia and a number of other laws including, for example, the Consumer Rights Protection Law (which protects consumers' rights when entering into contracts with manufacturers, traders or service providers), the Labour Law (regulating employment legal relationships), the Environmental Protection Law and the Law on Environmental Impact Assessment (regulating business's impact on the environment), and the Insolvency Law (which protects creditors' rights).

Reporting on stakeholder relations (Guideline V.B)

Guideline V.B recommends that listed or large SOEs report on stakeholder relations, including where relevant and feasible with regard to labour, creditors and affected communities. Latvian authorities stated that there is no formal requirement for SOEs to report on stakeholder relations.[70] However, Art. 55 of the Annual Accounts and Consolidated Annual Accounts Law requires large companies[71] to include in the management reports submitted with their annual accounts information on "non-financial indicators", including, for example, employee relations.[72] In practice, Latvian authorities state that some of Latvia's larger SOEs disclose information on stakeholder relations. Latvenergo, for example, reports on stakeholder relations on its website[73] and in its annual sustainability reports,[74] which are prepared in accordance with sustainability reporting guidelines developed by the Global Reporting Initiative.[75] The Ministry of Agriculture issues an annual forestry sector report that includes a report on engagement with stakeholders.

Internal controls, ethics and compliance programmes or measures (Guideline V.C)

Guideline V.C calls on SOE boards to develop, implement, monitor and communicate internal controls, ethics and compliance programmes or measures, including those which contribute to preventing fraud and corruption. In Latvia, there is no formal requirement for SOEs to develop internal codes of ethics, though some SOEs have begun doing so on their own initiative, including Air Baltic, Latvenergo, Latvijas

Attīstības finanšu institūcija, Latvijas Gaisa satiksme, Latvijas Loto, Latvijas Nacionālais Metroloģijas centrs, Latvijas Valsts ceļi, and Pasažieru vilciens. According to Latvian authorities, these compliance programmes sometimes include the establishment of a special ethics committee to review complaints and potential breaches of the code. For example, Pasažieru vilciens has an ethics committee that oversees application of the company's code of ethics and investigates possible violations of the code. The committee's three members are approved by the head of the management board and currently include representatives from Pasažieru vilciens' management board, legal department, and quality and security assurance department.

Board composition (Guideline VII.C)

Guideline VII.C recommends that SOEs' board composition allow the exercise of objective and independent judgment and that all board members – including any public officials – be nominated based on qualifications and have equivalent legal responsibilities. Prior to the entry into force of the PPCSCL, only five SOEs had supervisory boards. The CL governs the board composition and nomination criteria for four (Air Baltic Corporation, Lattelecom, LMT and Reverta); the board of Altum (the development finance institution) is subject to that SOE's statutory legislation.

As noted above, the PPCSCL introduced the option for large SOEs to re-establish supervisory boards after 1 January 2016. The government has committed to the re-establishment of these boards by end- 2016, according to regulations prepared by the Coordination Institution and adopted by the Cabinet between December 2015 and January 2016 on the nomination, size and composition, and remuneration of SOE supervisory and management boards. (For a list of all Coordination Institution guidelines and regulations under development as of end-2015, see Table 3.5. For more on supervisory board nominations see also section 3.3 above.)

Notes

1. Figures are as of end-2015, the latest available from Latvian authorities.

2. It should be noted that Latvian regulation also provides an additional protection for minority shareholders by prohibiting the controlling shareholder from exercising the right to vote on any shares that have exceeded the 50% threshold.

3. The disclosure of related party transactions is regulated under the Law on Annual Accounts, whose definition of "related parties" confirms with Regulation (EC) No 1606/2002 of the European Parliament and of the Council (International Accounting Standard 24). This definition is much broader than that included in CL 139[1] in that it includes *indirect* ownership or control of another entity via intermediaries in its definition.

4. See *www.europarl.europa.eu/sides/getDoc.do?pubRef=-//EP//TEXT+REPORT+A8-2015-0158+0+DOC+XML+V0//EN&language=en.*

5. Section 21.1 of the Criminal Law defines an organised group as "an association formed by more than two persons, which has been created for purposes of jointly committing criminal offences or serious or especially serious crimes and whose participants in accordance with previous agreement have divided responsibilities."

6. The annotations to Guidelines IV.A.2, VI.A.3 and VII.B and to Principles II.E.2 and V.A.3 of the *OECD Principles of Corporate Governance* recommend that information on shareholder agreements should be disclosed.

7. Article 5 of the Freedom of Information Law reads as follows:

   (1) Restricted access information is such information as is intended for a restricted group of persons in relation to the performance of their work or official duties and the disclosure or loss of which, due to the nature and content of such information, hinders or may hinder the activities of the institution, or causes or may cause harm to the lawful interests of persons.

   (2) As restricted access information shall be deemed information:

   (…)

   (3) which is a commercial secret, except in the case where a purchase contract has been entered into in accordance with the Public Procurement Law or other type of contract regarding actions with State or local government financial resources and property…

8. Notifications must be sent not later than two weeks before the meeting of shareholders (for LLCs) or not later than 30 days before the meeting (for JSCs). See Art. 214 for LLCs and Art. 273 for JSCs.

9. The Ministry of Transport owns 99.77% of Air Baltic. The remaining 0.23% of shares are held by (1) Russian airline company Transaero Airlines (0.228%); (2) Riga-based sole proprietorship SIA Frontier Enterprises (0.0002%), managed by Mr. Karl Gunther Sollinger, a former member of Air Baltic's supervisory board; and (3) Air Baltic, which reports that it owns 0.001% of shares.

10. See *www.reverta.lv/en/for-investors/shareholder-meetings*

11. An authorisation is not necessary for a person who represents the shareholder on the basis of law (e.g. the "ex officio" representative of a public authority). Such persons shall present a document certifying his or her right of representation. See CL Art. 212(3) (LLCs) and CL Art. 277(1) (JSCs).

12. TILTS Communications, which is indirectly owned by Sweden's TeliaSonera, owns 49% of Lattelecom shares.

13. The new Annual Accounts and Consolidated Annual Accounts Law entered into force on 1 January 2016 and replaces the former Annual Accounts Law and the Consolidated Annual Accounts Law. The law is meant to comply with the new EU Accounting Directive (Directive 2013/34/EU of European Parliament and of the Council of 26 June 2013 on the annual financial statements, consolidated financial statements and related reports of certain types of undertakings, amending Directive 2006/43/EC of the European Parliament and of the Council and repealing Council Directives 78/660/EEC and 83/349/EEC). It applies to financial statements for the financial year beginning on 1 January 2016 or during the calendar year 2016.

    The former Annual Accounts Law and the Consolidated Annual Accounts Law and also the new Annual Accounts and Consolidated Annual Accounts Law do not apply to banks, savings and loan societies, insurance commercial companies in the form of stock companies, mutual insurance co-operative societies, private pension funds, investment broker companies and investment management companies. Requirements for the annual accounts and consolidated annual accounts of banks and other financial institutions and for insurance and reinsurance companies are prescribed in the instructions and regulations of the Finance and Capital Market Commission.

14. Latvia Ministry of Economics (2009), *Annual Review of Latvian State-Owned Assets*, Riga.

15. For example, the Latvian authorities have described a confidential report prepared for the Ministry of Finance as part of a World Bank-organized Financial Reporting Technical Assistance Programme (FRTAP) in Latvia. The FRTAP report compared Latvian GAAP to IFRS to assess whether the application of one standard or the other would impact the calculation of corporate income tax. The Ministry of Finance is examining possibilities for allowing certain categories of taxpayers to carry out their accounting in accordance with international accounting standards. In parallel, authorities report that the Enterprise Income Tax Law is under evaluation in order to prevent the possibility that corporate entities reduce their taxable income "by using various accounting possibilities".

16. Since 2006 all parent companies in a company-group situation have had the option to apply consolidated financial statements according to IFRS under the former Consolidated Annual Accounts Law.

17. The new Law on Annual Reports and Consolidated Annual Reports applies the "large undertaking" size threshold included in the 2013 EU Accounting Directive 2013/34/EU. The Directive defines *large undertakings* as those entities whose balance sheets exceed at least two of the following three criteria in the preceding financial year: (1) balance sheet total of EUR 20 million, (2) net turnover of EUR 40 million, (3) 250 employees.

18. That said, SOEs that choose to apply IFRS to their accounts under Art. 3.7 of the Annual Accounts and Consolidated Annual Accounts Law will not be required to prepare two sets of accounts, one according to IFRS and one according to Latvian GAAP for the purposes of tax collection.

19. Since end-2014, two companies have delisted from the main list, bringing the total number of listed companies down to 27.

20. The largest four firms account for approximately 20% to 25% of sworn auditors in Latvia.

21. Directive 2014/56/EU (*http://eur-lex.europa.eu/legal-content/EN/TXT/?uri=celex:32014L0056)*.

22. Regulation 537/2014 (*http://eur-lex.europa.eu/legal-content/EN/TXT/PDF/?uri=CELEX:32014R0537).*

23. The size threshold for including non-financial indicators in management reports is provided under Art. 5.5 of the Annual Accounts and Consolidated Annual Accounts Law, which defines a large company as one that exceeds two of the following size criteria: a balance sheet total of EUR 20 million, a net turnover of EUR 40 million, and an average of 250 employees.

24. The State Revenue Service is "a direct administration authority under the supervision of the Minister for Finance, which ensures the accounting of tax payments and taxpayers, the collection of State taxes, fees and other mandatory payments specified by the State in the territory of the Republic of Latvia, as well as collects taxes, fees and other mandatory payments for the budget of the European Union, implements the

customs policy and organises customs matters." (Law on the State Revenue Service, Art. 1.)

25. According to Latvenergo's 2013 *Sustainability and Annual Report* (www.nasdaqomxbaltic.com/upload/reports/elek/2013_ar_en_uni_con_ias.pdf), Chair of the Management Board Āris Žīgurs received in total remuneration EUR 106 319; member Zane Kotāne received EUR 95 367; member Māris Kuņickis EUR 95 645; member Arnis Kurgs EUR 95 481; and member Uldis Bariss EUR 95 991.

For note, State forestry company Latvijas valsts meži only publishes combined remuneration figures for all four members of the management board. In 2010, the last year for which remuneration information is available, this figure totalled EUR 404 000.

26. Under the Law on Prevention of Conflict of Interest in the Activities of Public Officials, a public official has a duty to submit the following declarations within the time period specified and in accordance with the procedures specified: 1) a declaration to be submitted upon assuming the office; 2) a declaration for the current year; 3) a declaration to be submitted upon ending the duties of office; 4) a declaration to be submitted after the performance of duties of office has been terminated.

27. While the OECD Secretariat has not reviewed the Latvian regulation on SOE remuneration rates, Latvian authorities indicate that remuneration rates for management board members are set according to SOEs' size (large, medium and small – as defined according to size thresholds in the aforementioned 2013 EU Accounting Directive). Maximum monthly remuneration rates are calculated for each SOE size by multiplying the national average monthly salary (EUR 765 in 2014) by a coefficient set in the regulation. For example, the maximum remuneration rates for management board members of large SOE are calculated using a coefficient of 10. Remuneration of members of supervisory boards cannot exceed a coefficient of 3, capping monthly net director remuneration at not more than EUR 2 295.

28. The assessment was made in the government's June 2012 policy planning document, *Concept for Management of State Capital Shares* (www.em.gov.lv/em/2nd/?cat=30718). The document, along with a second parallel assessment, *Concept for Commercial Activities of Public Persons* (www.em.gov.lv/em/2nd/?cat=30718), provided an analytical background to the SOE sector reform initiative launched in 2011 that culminated in the adoption in 2014 of the PPCSCL. For more, see section A.7 of the *OECD Review of the Corporate Governance of State-Owned Enterprises in Latvia.*

29. The State Audit Office is an independent and autonomous government institution with funding allocated from the State budget. The Office reported that its forecasted budget for 2016 and 2017 will limit its ability to continue to take a systematic approach to SOE audits, which are often complex and require additional sectorial expertise. (The Office's budget remains 16% lower than pre-crisis levels: in 2008, the Office's allocated budget was EUR 6.6 million, which was then decreased by 42.8% in 2010. The 2016 budget is estimated to be EUR 5.5 million and at EUR 5.6 million for 2017.) Regarding the Office's overall resources, the 2015 OECD Economic Survey of Latvia recommends restoring the funding of the State Audit Office to at least pre-crisis levels as a means of improving public sector efficiency in the country. OECD (2015), *OECD Economic Surveys: Latvia 2015*, OECD Publishing, Paris, p. 81, https://www.oecd.org/eco/surveys/Overview_Latvia_2015_Eng.pdf.

30. The State Audit Office reported that, as of end-2014, it had performed 21 audits on the operations and management of state and local government capital companies, resulting in 408 audit recommendations, 335 of which were implemented and 14 of which are no longer applicable.

31. Available only in Latvian at the time of writing: *www.pkc.gov.lv/468-pkc-ir-sagatavojis-p%C4%81rskatu-par-valsts-kapit%C4%81lsabiedr%C4%ABb%C4%81m-un-valstij-piedero%C5%A1aj%C4%81m-kapit%C4%81la-da%C4%BC%C4%81m-2014-gad%C4%81.*

32. Latvian authorities report that this provision transposes into Latvian law the definition of beneficial ownership included in EU Directive 2005/60/EC (Art. 3, Paragraph 6).

33. The requirement to report this information to the Enterprise Register was introduced to the CL in 2011 to address anti-money laundering recommendations made by the Financial Action Task Force (FATF) and the Committee of Experts on the Evaluation of Anti-Money Laundering Measures and the Financing of Terrorism (MONEYVAL).

34. A company may be held liable under Art. 70^1 of the Criminal Law if the criminal offence was committed in the interests or for the benefit of the legal person, or as a result of lack of supervision or control by a natural person acting as an individual or as a member of "the collegial institution" of the company: (1) on the basis of a right to represent the legal person or to act on behalf of such legal person; (2) on the basis of taking decisions in the name of such legal person, (3) realising control within the scope of the legal person.

35. For example, the Public Utilities Commission (PUC) is responsible for enforcing the Law on Regulators of Public Utilities, and the Competition Council is responsible for enforcing the Competition Law. For more information on the application of these laws to SOEs, see section A.2.b of the *OECD Review of the Corporate Governance of State-Owned Enterprises in Latvia.*

36. Latvian authorities state that acquisition or divestment of state-owned property is governed by the Law on Alienation of the Property of a Public Person and the Law on Prevention of Squandering of the Financial Resources and Property of a Public Person. Property rights for state-owned real estate are governed by the Law on the State and Local Government Land Ownership Rights and Recording of Such Rights in Land Registers, as well as the Law on Recording of Immovable Property in the Land Registers. Finally, Cabinet Order No. 319 of 9 May 2006 requires ministries and other state governing bodies to eventually transfer state p to the State Real Estate Company, Valsts nekustamie īpašumi, which is an SOE owned by the Ministry of Finance.

37. While most of this core principle focuses on Guideline II, which recommends the clarification of the state's role as owner, Guidelines I.B and I.D recommend further clarification of how the State expects to carry out its role as owner by defining and disclosing its rationale for enterprise ownership. In doing so, these Guidelines help to establish whether the ownership function of the government is sufficiently developed and active to credibly handle the ownership function separately from regulation.

38. Latvian authorities explain that the definition of "assets" as used in Art. 88.1.3 of the SASL, while subject to interpretation by the Government and Parliament, could include railway infrastructure, airport infrastructure, electricity production,

transmission and distribution facilities, air navigation infrastructure, postal services network, and state-owned forests. Other examples of potentially strategically important assets, Latvian authorities add, could include telecommunications infrastructure and public road infrastructure.

39. The June 2013 report, coordinated by the Cross Sectoral Coordination Centre (CSCC), suggested significantly reducing state ownership, including (1) reorganising 16 SOEs as non-commercial public institutions, public agencies, or foundations; (2) merging nine SOEs; (3) divesting State ownership in 132 wholly-, majority- and minority-owned enterprises (including SOEs with the State's indirect participation); (4) liquidating 14 SOEs due to business inactivity, ongoing insolvency or bankruptcy processes; (5) and retaining state ownership in 77 enterprises. Recommendations in this regard were made based on a CSCC-led working group's opinion that State ownership in many cases was "unreasonable". In a number of cases, the working group found that SOEs had been created not according to the state enterprise ownership rationale under Latvian law, but either to supplement the State budget or to make them self-financing to decrease the State budget during the economic crisis.

40. Art. 10(3) of the State Administration Structure Law states that commercial activities undertaken by the State must be undertaken in the public interest. This provision circumscribes SOEs' commercial activity, which is defined under the CL as, "an open economic activity, which is performed by merchants in their name for the purposes of gaining a profit" (Art. 1.2).

41. Further information on identifying, costing, funding, and setting SOE commercial and non-commercial objectives can be found in Chapter 1 of the following report: OECD (2010), *Accountability and Transparency: A Guide for State Ownership*, OECD Publishing, Paris, *www.oecd.org/daf/ca /accountabilityandtransparencyaguideforstateownership.htm.*

42. Latvian Cabinet of Ministers (2012), *Concept for Management of State Capital Shares*, Riga.

43. For example, a 2013, the State Audit Office audit opinion of the implementation of the State and municipal 2012 budget found it was "not possible to gain assurance that the management of state and local government corporate enterprises is transparent and executed effectively, since no written document exists that governs the state policy concerning corporate enterprises, determining goals for state capital investment, and the methods and activities of state-owned enterprises with which to achieve these goals". State Audit Office (13 September 2013), "Opinion: Re. 2012 Annual Report of the Republic of Latvia on the implementation of the State budget and Municipal budgets, No.5.1-2-33/2012", Republic of Latvia State Audit Office, Riga, *www.lrvk.gov.lv/uploads/Majaslapa%20ENG/Audit%20report/2012/5.1-2-33_2012/atzinums_13092013_sgp_lav_eng-final.pdf.*

44. Art. 7 of the PPCSCL entered into force on 1 January 2016.

45. Some SOEs have recently approved or updated their medium-term operations strategies, and were therefore not required to submit new strategies to the Coordination Institution at the beginning of 2016. This is why, as stated above, the Coordination Institution expected strategies from only 42 SOEs. When these remaining SOEs' strategies expire or require updating, the SOEs will be required to submit their new strategies to the Coordination Institution for review. It should be noted that all 15 of Latvia's largest SOEs fall within this latter category of SOEs.

46. The Latvian Privatisation Agency (LPA) presentations made during (1) the 21 February 2014 introductory mission to Riga ("Better Governance of State-Owned Enterprises: Key Aspects of Reforms and Further Steps") and (2) the 3 April 2014 presentation to the Working Party ("Ownership Policy and Governance of SOEs in Latvia").

47. The CSCC operates under the Latvian Prime Minister. According to its website (*www.pkc.gov.lv/par-pkc/par-pkc*), the CSCC has 18 employees. Its overall responsibilities include ensuring implementation of Latvia's National Development Plan 2014-2020 and Sustainable Development Strategy through 2030; supervising and coordinating implementation of EU directives; performing analytical tasks assigned by the Office of the Prime Minister; and, more broadly, coordinating decision-making by Latvia's public administration.

48. As of January 2016, the line ministries indicated that, for the most part, their legal departments lead coordination with the Coordination Institution, sometimes with inputs from other operating units (i.e. the Ministries of Agriculture, Economy, Finance, and Health). The Ministry of Environmental Protection and Regional Department is responsible for SOE-related matters in each of its operating units, while the Latvian Privatisation Agency, the Ministry of Culture, and the Ministry of Transportation have divisions dedicated to state enterprise ownership matters.

49. Employees from the CSCC Development Planning Division will be temporarily seconded to the Coordination Institution unit in early 2016 for the purposes of assisting with the assessment of SOEs' medium-term operations strategies, particularly the evaluation of non-commercial objectives.

50. See *http://tap.mk.gov.lv/lv/mk/tap/?pid=40329622&mode=mk&date=2014-09-23* (an unofficial English translation of the resolution is available from the Secretariat).

51. This includes, for example, preferential financing, tax arrears or other preferential trade credits from other SOEs. It can also include SOEs' receiving inputs (such as energy, water or land) at prices or conditions more favourable than those available to private competitors.

52. Latvijas Dzelzceļš' consolidated financial reports state that net profits decreased from EUR 40 253 in 2007 to EUR -3 183 in 2010. Returns on assets and on equity decreased from 0.40% and 1% in 2009 (the earliest year this information is available), respectively, to -0.5% and -1.30% in 2010.

53. Section 3.5, "Public Procurement," in EBRD, *Commercial Laws of Latvia, October 2011: An Assessment by the EBRD*, Office of the General Counsel, EBRD, London, www.ebrd.com/downloads/sector/legal /latvia.pdf.

54. *www.saeima.lv/en/legislation/constitution.*

55. *www.oecd.org/investment/investment-policy/oecddeclarationanddecisions.htm.*

56. *www.oecd.org/corporate/mne.*

57. See section B.2.b of the OECD Working Group on Bribery's 2015 *Phase 2 evaluation of Latvia's implementation of the OECD Anti-Bribery Convention* (OECD, Paris), *www.oecd.org/daf/anti-bribery/Latvia-Phase-2-Report-ENG.pdf.*

58. Section 9 of the Labour Law protects an employee who, within the scope of a legal employment relationship, "informs competent authorities regarding suspicions about

the commission of criminal offences or administrative violations in the workplace." In the event of a dispute, the employer must prove that his/her actions were justified. Damages are available as a remedy.

59. Juris Dreifelds and Valts Kalninš (2014), *Latvia*, Freedom House, Washington DC, www.freedomhouse.org/report/nations-transit/2014/latvia.

60. The OECD Working Group on Bribery's *Phase 2 evaluation of Latvia's implementation of the OECD Anti-Bribery Convention* also recommends that Latvia work to comprehensively protect public and private sector whistle-blowers. See p. 72: www.oecd.org/daf/anti-bribery/Latvia-Phase-2-Report-ENG.pdf.

61. World Bank. 2013. *Doing Business 2014: Understanding Regulations for Small and Medium-Size Enterprises,* World Bank Group, Washington DC, http://dx.doi.org/10.1596/978-0-8213-9984-2. (Reference to Latvia's insolvency framework: www.doingbusiness.org/data/exploreeconomies/latvia?topic=resolving-insolvency#resolving-insolvency)

62. European Commission Directorate-General for Justice (2015), 2015 EU Justice Scoreboard, http://ec.europa.eu/justice/effective-justice/scoreboard/index_en.htm. The EU report described this indicator as a measure of the time required for creditors to recover their credit. The period of time was measured based on a hypothetical case tracking the time required from the company's default until the payment of some or all of the money owed to the bank. Potential delay tactics by the parties, such as the filing of dilatory appeals or request for extension, are taken into consideration. The data are collected from questionnaire responses by local insolvency practitioners and verified through a study of laws and regulations as well as public information on bankruptcy systems.

63. The number of announced insolvency proceedings involving natural persons increased sharply through 2013, while the number of completed proceedings remained a small fraction of the total. For cases involving legal persons, the big increase in insolvency cases occurred in 2009-10, whereas in more recent years the number of cases initiated each year has dropped substantially, allowing for a much closer alignment with the number of cases initiated each year.

64. FICIL (2015).

65. Latvia State Audit Office (19 March 2015), "Is the State's Insolvency Policy Effective?", unofficial translation, State Audit Office, Riga.

66. The September 2015 FICIL position paper also cites the results of a business survey conducted by the Latvian Chamber of Commerce and Industry in which 80% of surveyed entrepreneurs believe that insolvency proceedings are not conducted properly and transparently, 56% say they have been victims of insolvency abuse themselves, and 75% of those who say they have been victims of insolvency abuse report that there were no negative consequences for the abusers.

67. The working group consists of (1) the Association of the Certified Administrators of Insolvency Proceedings of Latvia, (2) the Association of Borrowers of Latvia, (3) the State Revenue Service, (4) the Foreign Investors' Council in Latvia, (5) the Ministry of Economics, (6) the Association of Commercial Banks of Latvia, (7) the Employers' Confederation of Latvia, (8) the Free Trade Union Confederation of Latvia, (9) the Latvian Council of Sworn Advocates, (10) the Latvian Sworn Bailiff Board, (11) the Latvian Chamber of Commerce and Industry, (12) the Ministry of

Finance, (13) the Riga District Court, (14) the Supreme Court of the Republic of Latvia and (15) the Insolvency Administration.

68. Ministry of Justice submission to the OECD Secretariat on 18 August 2014 titled "Court Cases Heard by the Senate (Cassation instance in the Supreme Court) 2010-2014".

69. World Bank (2002), *Report on the Observance of Standards and Codes (ROSC): Corporate Governance Country Assessment of the Republic of Latvia,* World Bank, Washington DC..

70. For note, listed companies traded on the Nasdaq Riga exchange are required to apply Section 10 of the Nasdaq Riga Principles of Corporate Governance, which focuses on investor relations and includes engaging with and informing "other interested parties: employees, creditors and business partners".

71. Large companies are defined under Art. 5.5 of the Annual Accounts and Consolidated Annual Accounts Law as those that exceed two of the following three size criteria: a balance sheet total of EUR 20 million, net turnover of EUR 40 million, and an average of 250 employees.

72. For more on disclosure requirements under this law see section 3.2.

73. www.latvenergo.lv/eng/corporate_social_responsibility/cooperation_with_stakeholders.

74. www.latvenergo.lv/eng/corporate_social_responsibility/sustainability_report.

75. www.globalreporting.org/standards/g4/Pages/default.aspx.

References

Dreifelds, Juris, and Valts Kalninš (2014), *Latvia*, Freedom House, Washington DC, www.freedomhouse.org/report/nations-transit/2014/latvia.

EBRD, Commercial Laws of Latvia (2011), An Assessment by the EBRD, Office of the General Counsel, October, EBRD, London, www.ebrd.com/downloads/sector/legal/latvia.pdf.

European Commission Directorate-General for Justice (2015), *2015 EU Justice Scoreboard,* European Commission, Brussels, http://ec.europa.eu/justice/effective-justice/scoreboard/index_en.htm.

FICIL (Foreign Investors' Council in Latvia) (2015), *Position Paper on the Insolvency Process,* FICIL, Riga, www.ficil.lv/f/15%2009%2024%20Insolvency%20Process.pdf.

FICIL (2013), *Proposals for Facilitating Efficiency of the Court System*, FICIL, Riga, www.ficil.lv/view/en/22/proposals-for-facilitating-efficiency-of-the-court-system-2013.

FISIL (2011), *Position Paper on Capital Markets Development*, FICIL, Riga, www.ficil.lv/f/11%2005%2020%20On_Capital_Markets.pdf.

IMF (2013), *Republic of Latvia: 2012 Article IV Consultation and Second Post-Program Monitoring Discussions*, Country Report, No. 13/28, IMF, Washington DC, www.imf.org/external/pubs/ft/scr/2013/cr1328.pdf.

Latvia Cabinet of Ministers (2012), *Concept for Management of State Capital Shares*, Riga.

Latvia Cabinet of Ministers (2009), *Annual Review of Latvian State-Owned Assets*, Riga, p. 76.

Latvia Ministry of Economics (2015), *Economic Development of Latvia*, Ministry of Economics of the Republic of Latvia, Riga, *https://www.em.gov.lv/en/economic_development/report_on_the_economic_development_of_latvia.*

Latvia Ministry of Economics (2009), *Annual Review of Latvian State-Owned Assets*, Ministry of Economics of the Republic of Latvia, Riga.

Latvia Ministry of Justice (2014), "Court Cases Heard by the Senate (Cassation instance in the Supreme Court) 2010-2014", submission to the OECD Secretariat on 18 August 2014.

Latvia State Audit Office (2013), "Opinion: Re. 2012 Annual Report of the Republic of Latvia on the implementation of the State budget and Municipal budgets, No.5.1-2-33/2012", 13 September, Republic of Latvia State Audit Office, Riga, *www.lrvk.gov.lv/uploads/Majaslapa%20ENG/Audit%20report/2012/5.1-2-33_2012/atzinums_13092013_sgp_lav_eng-final.pdf*

Latvia State Audit Office (2015), "Is the State's Insolvency Policy Effective?", 19 March, unofficial translation, State Audit Office, Riga.

Nasdaq Baltic (2016), *Review of Corporate Governance Practices in the Baltics, www.nasdaqbaltic.com/files/baltic/CG%20review/Review%20of%20CG%20practices%20in%20the%20Baltics%20in%202015.pdf.*

Nasdaq Baltic (2015), *Promoting Baltic Economic Growth through IPOs: Study and Action Proposals, www.nasdaqbaltic.com/files/baltic/IPO_TF/0816-Q15%20Economic%20growth%20IPO_BALTIC_Eng_FNL.pdf.*

Nasdaq Baltic (2015), *Review of Corporate Governance Practices in the Baltics in 2015, www.nasdaqbaltic.com/files/baltic/CG%20review/Review%20of%20CG%20practices%20in%20the%20Baltics%20in%202015.pdf.*

Nasdaq OMX Riga (2014), *NASDAQ OMX Riga Rules on Listing and Trading of Financial Instruments on the Markets Regulated by the Exchange, www.nasdaqomxbaltic.com/files/riga/rules/NQRiga_Eng/2014_10_06_RSE_Listing_KONSOLIDETIE_T+2_ENG.pdf.*

Nasdaq OMX Riga (2010), *Principles of Corporate Governance and Recommendations on their Implementation, www.nasdaqomxbaltic.com/files/riga/corp_gov_May_2010_final_EN.pdf.*

OECD (2015a), *G20/OECD Principles of Corporate Governance*, OECD Publishing, Paris. *http://dx.doi.org/10.1787/9789264236882-en.*

OECD (2015b), *OECD Economic Surveys: Latvia 2015, https://www.oecd.org/eco/surveys/Overview_Latvia_2015_Eng.pdf.*

OECD (2015c), *OECD Guidelines on Corporate Governance of State-Owned Enterprises,* 2015 Edition, OECD Publishing, Paris, *http://dx.doi.org/10.1787/9789264244160-en .*

OECD (2015d), *Recommendation of the Council on Principles of Corporate Governance*, *http://acts.oecd.org/Instruments/ShowInstrumentView.aspx?InstrumentID=322&InstrumentPID=358&Lang=en&Book=False.*

OECD (2015e), *Recommendation of the Council on Guidelines on Corporate Governance of State-Owned Enterprises*, *http://acts.oecd.org/Instruments/ShowInstrumentView.aspx?InstrumentID=323&InstrumentPID=359&Lang=en&Book=False.*

OECD (2015f), *OECD Review of the Corporate Governance of State-Owned Enterprises in Latvia*, www.oecd.org/daf/ca/oecd-review-corporate-governance-soe-latvia.htm.

OECD (2014), *The Size and Sectoral Distribution of SOEs in OECD and Partner Countries*, OECD Publishing, Paris, *http://dx.doi.org/10.1787/9789264215610-en*

OECD (2013), *Roadmap for the Accession of Latvia to the OECD Convention*, *www.oecd.org/officialdocuments/publicdisplaydocumentpdf/?cote=C(2013)122/FINAL&docLanguage=En.*

OECD Working Group on Bribery (2015), *Phase 2 evaluation of Latvia's implementation of the OECD Anti-Bribery Convention*, *www.oecd.org/daf/anti-bribery/Latvia-Phase-2-Report-ENG.pdf.*

World Bank (2002), Report on the Observance of Standards and Codes (ROSC): Corporate Governance Country Assessment of the Republic of Latvia, World Bank, Washington DC, *http://documents.worldbank.org/curated/en/892401468266155910/Latvia-Republic-of-Report-on-the-Observance-of-Standards-and-Codes-ROSC-Corporate-Governance-Country-Assessment*

Chapter 4

Conclusions and recommendations for Latvia's corporate governance framework

This report provides an assessment of Latvia's corporate governance framework for listed and state-owned enterprises with respect to five "core corporate governance principles" set out in the Roadmap for the Accession of Latvia to the OECD Convention, which in turn draws upon the G20/OECD Principles of Corporate Governance ("the Principles") and the G20/OECD Corporate Governance of State-Owned Enterprises ("the Guidelines").

As suggested by its title, this final chapter has two parts. First, it presents the ***conclusions of assessments*** *made by the OECD Corporate Governance Committee and the OECD Working Party on State Ownership and Privatisation Practices of Latvia's position relative to the Principles and the Guidelines, respectively. Second, it provides a* ***set of recommendations*** *by which Latvia may further align its framework with these instruments.*

This report provides an assessment of Latvia's corporate governance framework for listed and state-owned enterprises with respect to five "core corporate governance principles" set out in the *Roadmap for the Accession of Latvia to the OECD Convention*, which draws upon the *Recommendation of the Council on the Principles of Corporate Governance* (Principles) and the *Recommendation of the Guidelines on Corporate Governance of State-Owned Enterprises* (Guidelines). This chapter has two parts. First, it presents the conclusions of assessments made by the OECD Corporate Governance Committee and the OECD Working Party on State Ownership and Privatisation Practices of Latvia's position relative to the Principles and the Guidelines, respectively. Second, it provides a set of recommendations by which Latvia may further align its framework with these instruments.

4.1. Conclusions

This report reaches a positive overall view of Latvia's corporate governance framework in relation to the recommendations in the Principles. While some weaknesses were also identified, the Latvian government has responded to most concerns via new and/or pending legislation and other reforms. The report also recognises important steps taken by the government to address serious concerns raised by the Working Party regarding Latvia's framework for the corporate governance of Latvian SOEs. The following are some of the key issues, strengths and weaknesses of Latvia's corporate governance framework and implementation:

- ***Latvia's corporate governance landscape:*** Latvia's legal and regulatory framework for the corporate governance of listed companies is largely consistent with the Principles. The practical reality, however, is that Latvia's capital market is small. Certain steps would strengthen and support a deepening of the market, including (1) strengthening the enforcement of, as well as sanctions for, rules against market misconduct, including insider trading; (2) strengthening the efficiency of judicial review of commercial cases; (3) reviewing the impact of Latvia's insolvency framework; (4) strengthening the framework for supervising and disclosing related party transactions; and (5) clarifying the role and composition of the audit committee. It is encouraging to note that the Latvian government is already working to address these challenges via a wide range of reforms, which they have shown a strong commitment to enacting. The picture with respect to corporate governance of state-owned enterprises is more complex because, at the time of writing, the government was in the early stages of implementing major SOE reforms enacted in 2014 and amended in 2015. If implemented effectively, the new SOE governance law, the Public Persons Capital Shares and Companies Law (PPCSCL), would address many of the weaknesses earlier identified by the Working Party. Significantly, the PPCSCL establishes a state enterprise ownership coordination function, and it encourages large, commercially oriented SOEs to re-establish boards of directors. A March 2016 government decree further obligates Latvia's largest commercial SOEs to re-establish supervisory boards by end-2016, complemented by the inclusion of this commitment in Latvia's Final Statement accepting the obligations of OECD membership. The Final Statement will become part of the Accession Agreement with the OECD, which is an international agreement ratified by Latvia's parliament. Other reforms the PPCSCL introduces include requirements to clarify SOE commercial and non-commercial objectives and strategies and to enhance disclosure and reporting.

- ***Ensuring the enforcement of shareholder rights and equitable treatment:*** Latvia's legal framework appears to broadly provide for the protection and facilitation of the exercise of shareholder rights in accordance with the Principles' recommendations, though some cases of abuse of shareholder rights have been noted. The government has recognized the need to protect minority shareholder rights and is taking steps to strengthen measures in this regard. A key reform priority currently under consideration by a Ministry of Justice-led working group must be to strengthen and clarify the framework for supervising and disclosing related party transactions. For SOEs, few have non-state investors with shareholdings larger than 5%. That said, non-state shareholders' rights appear to be respected, though more could be done to adequately disclose to non-state shareholders information on SOEs' public policy objectives.

- ***Timely and reliable disclosure in accordance with international standards:*** Latvia's framework for listed companies generally meets the Principles' recommendations with respect to international accounting and auditing standards. International Financial Reporting Standards (IFRS) are required for Latvia's main tier of listed companies, while many of the second-tier listed companies also follow IFRS. Latvia's SOEs have also implemented most of the Guidelines' recommendations on disclosure, including the first aggregate report on SOEs issued by the Coordination Institution on 16 February 2016. However, reporting according to IFRS remains a concern. In 2014, the Working Party recommended Latvia require at least large SOEs to apply IFRS because of concerns that Latvian Generally Accepted Accounting Principles (GAAP) may not be equivalent to IFRS in their ability to provide a true valuation of SOEs' assets and liabilities. As of 1 January 2016, SOEs legally have the option to choose to apply IFRS to their annual and consolidated annual reports, under the new Annual Accounts and Consolidated Annual Accounts Law. Fourteen of Latvia's 15 large SOEs report that they plan to apply IFRS to their accounts under the new Law. Regarding the disclosure of governance, ownership and voting structures, Latvia's rules are generally consistent with the Principles' and the Guidelines' other disclosure recommendations. This report also highlights shortcomings regarding the framework for the supervision and disclosure of related party transactions, which, as noted above, the Latvian government has committed to addressing through legislation to be developed by September 2016.

- ***Effective separation of the government's role as owner and its regulatory role:*** As of early 2016, a number of key provisions from the PPCSCL had just entered into force and supporting regulations and guidance were just beginning to be applied. It will remain essential to ensure that these provisions are effectively implemented in order to address a number of the weaknesses identified in this review, including the blurring of the distinction between the state's ownership function and other state functions that could influence conditions for Latvian SOEs. This must include re-introducing effective and professional supervisory boards in all large commercially-oriented SOEs by the end of 2016, and ensuring that the new Coordination Institution has the resources and authority to effectively coordinate the exercise of the state enterprise ownership function as per the PPCSCL.

- ***Ensuring a level playing field:*** According to the Latvian authorities, SOEs do not receive any preferential treatment from the government. The review also did not find evidence of significant challenges faced by stakeholders seeking redress. Latvia's framework governing SOEs' involvement in public procurement contracting also appears in line with OECD recommendations in this area. Where Latvia could strengthen its framework is in regard to practices for identifying and disclosing public policy objectives and related costs. Provisions introduced under the PPCSCL requiring the Coordination Institution to work with line ministries and SOEs to publish information regarding public policy objectives, including their associated costs and their achievement, could address concerns in this area. In addition, as noted above, at least large SOEs should apply IFRS to their financial accounts, due to questions surrounding Latvian GAAP and their ability to provide a true valuation of SOEs' assets.

- ***Recognising stakeholder rights and the duties, rights and responsibilities of boards:*** The framework for establishing stakeholders' rights as set forth in Latvian law generally reflects OECD recommendations. Measures for seeking redress for the violation of stakeholders' rights may be improving with recent reforms to Latvia's court system and the introduction of new laws on arbitration and mediation. At the time of writing, the government was also developing a new law introducing whistle-blower protections for both private and public sector employees. The government is also working to strengthen its framework for assessing and monitoring implementation of recent insolvency reforms. With respect to boards of listed companies, Latvia's two-tiered board structure generally follows most OECD recommendations related to the duties, rights and responsibilities of supervisory boards, including in relation to stakeholders. Once established, the effectiveness of new SOE boards will need to be assessed. However, the Latvian government has issued regulations and guidance regarding board nomination criteria and procedures, and government ministries reported that they would establish boards in 12 large SOEs beginning in the second quarter of 2016 to be fully phased in by the end of 2016.

4.2. Recommendations

The Committee and the Working Party note that Latvia has made progress in its implementation of the Principles and the Guidelines. Nevertheless, they have identified areas where further improvements are recommended following accession to the Organisation.

Priority recommendations

Specifically, the following **priority recommendations** have been identified for the Committee and Working Party to monitor and assess through a requirement for follow-up reporting to ensure the implementation of the OECD's corporate governance instruments:

- To ensure effective separation of the regulatory and ownership functions for state-owned enterprises and to further implement the Recommendation *of the Council on Guidelines on Corporate Governance of State-Owned Enterprises*, Latvia should:
  - Follow through on its pledge to establish professional boards of directors in all large commercial SOEs, based on the application of clear selection and nomination procedures for SOE board members. The Committee notes that Latvia has agreed to make a legally binding commitment to implement this

recommendation by the end of 2016, by including it in its Final Statement accepting the obligations of OECD membership. The Final Statement will become part of the Accession Agreement with the OECD, which is an international agreement ratified by Latvia's parliament.

- Build on progress made in 2015 to strengthen the performance of its ownership function by, before the end of 2016, taking clear steps to ensure the effective implementation of the Public Persons Capital Shares and Companies Law (PPCSCL) and its implementing regulations and guidelines. This should encompass (1) the development, review and monitoring by line ministries, in cooperation with the Coordination Institution, of SOEs' medium-term operations strategies, including the clarification therein of SOEs' commercial and non-commercial objectives; and (2) the development of future annual aggregate reports.
- Ensure that the 13 of Latvia's largest SOEs which have committed to apply International Financial Reporting Standards (IFRS) to their individual and consolidated (where applicable) annual accounts beginning with the 2016 annual reporting period, follow through on this commitment. As required for listed companies on Latvia's main listing segment, all large commercial SOEs should choose to apply IFRS to their financial accounts on the basis of the new 2015 Annual Accounts and Consolidated Annual Accounts Law.

• To ensure the enforcement of shareholder rights and equitable shareholder treatment, Latvia should address weaknesses identified in the framework for treatment and disclosure of related party transactions by enacting necessary legislation to strengthen this framework by the end of 2016.

In addition, the Committee and Working Party have identified the following additional recommendations, for which Latvia is invited to provide progress reports in the context of regular reporting to the Committee and its Working Party.

Additional recommendations related to Latvia's implementation of the Principles:

It is recommended that Latvia:

• *Strengthen its corporate governance framework for listed companies.* Latvia should continue the progress it has made in strengthening the efficiency of judicial review of commercial cases. The government should also continue its assessment of its insolvency framework. In addition, Latvia should enact legislative proposals to amend the Financial Instruments Markets Law (FIML) to strengthen the enforcement capacity of the Financial and Capital Market Commission (FCMC) and to clarify the role, composition and functioning of the audit committee.

• *Improve enforcement and establish whistle-blower protections.* Latvia should continue efforts to strengthen the effectiveness and coordination of the enforcement of cases of market misconduct, including insider trading; this will be integral to deepening confidence in Latvia's capital markets. These efforts should also include establishing appropriate channels for whistle-blowing and protections for whistle-blowers, given the important role whistle-blowers can play in identifying misconduct.

Additional recommendations related to Latvia's implementation of the Guidelines:

It is recommended that Latvia:

- *Effectively coordinate and exercise the state ownership function.* The establishment of the Coordination Institution has the potential to facilitate the more effective exercise of the state enterprise ownership function in Latvia. The government should ensure that the Coordination Institution is equipped with the human and financial resources sufficient for it to fulfil all of its responsibilities under the PPCSCL. At the same time, line ministries should also demonstrate they are committed to cooperating with the Coordination Institution.
- *Clarify the state ownership policy and ownership objectives.* Amendments to the State Administration Structure Law, adopted on 22 October 2015, streamline conditions for state enterprise ownership. In implementing the new ownership policy, the government should clarify and communicate the criteria to be applied in order to identify which services, goods and properties are "of strategic importance" and how state enterprise ownership may be justified "in protection of the public interest".
- *Consider establishing boards in remaining commercial SOEs.* Professional supervisory boards serve as a cornerstone of good corporate governance for commercially oriented SOEs. Latvia should therefore review experience gained in establishing boards in its large SOEs in order to consider their expansion to all remaining commercial SOEs, regardless of size

References

OECD (2015a), *G20/OECD Principles of Corporate Governance*, OECD Publishing, Paris. *http://dx.doi.org/10.1787/9789264236882-en*.

OECD (2015b), *OECD Guidelines on Corporate Governance of State-Owned Enterprises,* 2015 Edition, OECD Publishing, Paris, *http://dx.doi.org/10.1787/9789264244160-en*.

OECD (2013), *Roadmap for the Accession of Latvia to the OECD Convention,* *www.oecd.org/officialdocuments/publicdisplaydocumentpdf/?cote=C(2013)122/FINAL&docLanguage=En*.

ANNEX A

Latvian state-owned enterprises

In the following table, data provided by the Latvian authorities is current through 2014, and all financial figures are in euros and consolidated.

SOE name	% state-owned	Share-holder	Sector	Statutory capital (EUR)	Balance sheet total (EUR)	Net turnover (EUR)	Profit/losses (EUR)	Employ-ees
Sertifikācijas un testēšanas centrs	100	LPA	Certification	335 798	447 909	656 064	-2,515	28
Lattelecom Subsidiaries: LLC Lattelecom Technology (100%); LLC Lattelecom BPO (23%); LLC Citrus Solutions (23%); LLC Baltijas Datoru Akadēmija (indirectly); LLC BPO Baltic (netieši) (23%); LLC Latvijas Mobilais Telefons (50%); JSC Pirmais slēgtais pensiju fonds	51	LPA	Communi-cations	207 851 691	323 624 000	188 014 000	30 079 000	1 912
Latvijas Mobilais Telefons Subsidiaries: LLC ZetCOM (100%); LLC LMT Retail&Logistics (100%)	5	LPA	Communi-cations	817 013	230 277 073	161 177 091	22 077 783	868
Reverta Subsidiaries: Parex Leasing & Factoring; Regalite Holdings Limited; UAB NIF Lietuva; OU NIF Eesti; SIA NIF Dzīvojamie Īpašumi; SIA NIF Komercīpašumi; SIA NIF Zemes Īpašumi; SIA NIF Projekts 1, SIA NIF Projekts 6, SIA NIF Projekts 7, SIA NIF Projekts 8; Carnella Maritime Corp	84.15	LPA	Real estate/non-performing loans	442 552 000	228 820 000		-60 389 000	
Zemkopības ministrijas nekustamie īpašumi	100	MoA	Real estate	3 422 007	7 002 604	4 539 035	3 095	150
Meliorprojekts	100	MoA	Water management	115 691	271 721	458 757	5 742	30
Latvijas Valsts meži Subsidiaries: LLC "Jaunmoku pils" (100%), LLC "Meža un koksnes produktu pētniecības un attīstības institūts" (40%), JSC "Latvijas finieris" (0,82%)	100	MoA	Forest management	264 052 390	367 097 733	275 717 148	75 453 799	1 272
"Latvijas Lauku konsultāciju un izglītības centrs"	99.08	MoA	Agriculture	844 326	4 573 148	7 544 612	9 885	454
Mihaila Čehova Rīgas Krievu teātris	100	MoC	Culture	2 846	460 581	2 492 099	-134 038	128
Daugavpils teātris	100	MoC	Culture	2 846	122 249	136 387	30 279	

SOE name	% state-owned	Share-holder	Sector	Statutory capital (EUR)	Balance sheet total (EUR)	Net turnover (EUR)	Profit/losses (EUR)	Employ-ees
Valmieras drāmas teātris	100	MoC	MoC	2 846	467 014	623 619	2 665	
Latvijas Nacionālais teātris	100	MoC	MoC	2 846	1 270 443	3 676 261	2 049	
Dailes teātris	100	MoC	MoC	14 229	961 013	3 561 900	-13 195	
Latvijas Leļļu teātris	100	MoC	Culture	2 846	288 301	532 230	11 521	
Valsts Akadēmiskais koris "Latvija"	100	MoC	Culture	2 846	331 367	1 020 034	1 841	
Latvijas Nacionālais simfoniskais orķestris	100	MoC	Culture	2 846	726 671	528 325	5 089	
KREMERATA BALTICA	100	MoC	Culture	2 846	54 304	739 527	736	
Latvijas Koncerti	100	MoC	Culture	2 846	1 161 029	1 192 240	41 930	
Jaunais Rīgas teātris	100	MoC	Culture	42 144	998 945	2 278 586	27 307	101
Rīgas cirks	100	MoC	Culture	3 073	362 771	899 103	141 581	
Latvijas Nacionālā opera	100	MoC	Culture	96 755	6 401 736	11 107 470	126 489	
Liepājas simfoniskais orķestris	100	MoC	Culture	58 053	307 809	187 963	25 902	
Latvenergo Subsidiaries: LLC "LIEPĀJAS ENERĢIJA" (51%); JSC "Latvijas elektriskie tīkli" (100%); JSC "Sadales tīkls" (100%); JSC "Enerģijas publiskais tirgotājs" (100%); JSC "Rīgas siltums" (0.0051%); JSC "Pirmais Slēgtais Pensiju Fonds" (46.3%);	100	MoE	Energy	1 288 446 358	3 486 576 259	1 010 757 499	28 514 810	4 559
Privatizācijas aģentūra Subsidiaries: LLC "Hiponia"(100%) JSC "Reverta" (84.15%)	100	MoE	Real estate capital shares	422 405 747	151 451 418	3 046 548	-129 792 622	67
Latvijas Nacionālais metroloģijas centrs	100	MoE	Calibration and verification of measuring instruments	633 463	1 168 596	1 210 810	9 266	78
Standartizācijas akreditācijas un metroloģijas centrs	100	MoE	Standards and accreditation	162 925	670 891	734 808	56 341	38
Latvijas Vides ģeoloģijas un meteoroloģijas centrs	100	MoEPRD	Environment	25 303 641	20 979 987	5 947 016	-523 975	295
Vides investīciju fonds	100	MoEPRD	Finance	6 229 332	6 831 623	680 384	10 906	8
VSIA Vides projekti[0]	100	MoEPRD	Environment					
Elektroniskie sakari	100	MoEPRD	Communi-cations	8 721 583	11 487 632	5 541 845	6 714	99
Rīgas Tūrisma un radošās industrijas tehnikums	100	MoES	Education	5 836 620	11 742 408	4 604 868	21 605	298
Bobsleja un kamaniņu trase "Sigulda"	100	MoES	Sports	4 714 785	6 549 554	656 279	-53 371	35
Bulduru dārzkopības vidusskola	100	MoES	Education	2 898 389	6 021 587	1 910 291	503 757	96
Kultūras un sporta centrs „Daugavas stadions"	100	MoES	Sports	17135	940 727	270 579	1 594	21
Sporta centrs „Mežaparks'	99.99	MoES	Sports	15 604 420	15 713 112	226 478	-9 659	15
Tenisa centrs „Lielupe"	99.99	MoES	Sports	11 164 042	12 014 639	219 835	53 464	15
Valsts nekustamie īpašumi Subsidiaries: LLC "VNĪ pilis" (100%); LLC "Veselības aprūpes nekustamie īpašumi" (100%); LLC "Biroju Centrs Ezerparks" (31.5%)	100	MoF	Real estate	135 415 906	344 369 157	51 719 725	2 499 808	573

SOE name	% state-owned	Share-holder	Sector	Statutory capital (EUR)	Balance sheet total (EUR)	Net turnover (EUR)	Profit/losses (EUR)	Employ-ees
Latvijas Proves birojs	100	MoF	Verification of precious metals and jewellery	746 333	671 837	499 579	21 737	18
Latvijas Loto Subsidiaries: LLC "Latloto nams" (100%)	100	MoF	Lotteries	284 574	11 408 110	21 966 648	3 533 103	102
Augstsprieguma tīkls Subsidiaries: JSC "Nord Pool Spot" (2%); JSC "Pirmais slēgtais pensiju fonds" (1.9%)	100	MoF	Energy	5 691 487	77 492 027	110 502 757	998 309	505
Attīstības finanšu institūcija Altum Subsidiaries: LLC "Riska investīciju sabiedrība" (100%)	100	MoF (40%) MoE (30%) MoA (30%)	Finance	204 862 333	443 702 000	5 620 000	95 000	298
Traumatoloģijas un ortopēdijas slimnīca	100	MoH	Healthcare	3 947 044	11 055 579	11 464 949	76 176	456
Piejūras slimnīca	100	MoH	Healthcare	699 475	10 926 641	3 142 278	-96 041	222
Rīgas Psihiatrijas un narkoloģijas centrs	100	MoH	Healthcare	4 432 385	25 950 441	11 347 623	2 090	886
Daugavpils psihoneiroloģiskā slimnīca	100	MoH	Healthcare	504 906	18 508 411	6 699 629	20 030	597
Strenču psihoneiroloģiskā slimnīca	100	MoH	Healthcare	295 550	7 204 455	4 365 849	119 218	348
Bērnu psihoneiroloģiskā slimnīca "Ainaži"	100	MoH	Healthcare	60 236	4 446 687	1 091 181	44 857	95
Aknīstes psihoneiroloģiskā slimnīca	100	MoH	Healthcare	277 460	7 031 451	3 225 400	31 752	291
Slimnīca „Ģintermuiža	100	MoH	Healthcare	2 099 164	14 542 410	5 019 846	8 453	488
Bērnu klīniskā universit+A65ātes slimnīca	100	MoH	Healthcare	3 983 954	60 696 007	32 576 002	141 359	2 030
Nacionālais rehabilitācijas centrs "Vaivari"	100	MoH	Healthcare	793 677	9 788 911	8 280 384	86 522	452
Straupes narkoloģiskā slimnīca	100	MoH	Healthcare	90 525	159 776	570 006	-27 412	58
Rīgas Austrumu klīniskā universitātes slimnīca Subsidiaries: LLC "Rīgas Hematoloģijas centrs" (51%); LLC "Veselības centrs „Biķernieki"" (99.6%)	100	MoH	Healthcare	15 681 429	101 731 230	89 288 360	-8 759 987	4 893
Paula Stradiņa klīniskā universitātes slimnīca	100	MoH	Healthcare	19 366 829	103 841 466	83 157 729	147 333	2 993
Iekšlietu ministrijas poliklīnika	100	MoI	Healthcare	556 395	810 232	1 846 826	19 318	129
Latvijas Vēstnesis	100	MoJ	Justice	711 436	2 924 080	918 507	69 274	64
Tiesu namu aģentūra	100	MoJ	Justice	27 169 649	49 095 930	2 928 983	119 705	108
Latvijas dzelzceļš Subsidiaries: LLC "LDZ CARGO" (100%); LLC "LDZ ritošā sastāva serviss" (100%); LLC "LDZ infrastruktūra" (100%); LLC "LDZ apsardze" (100%); JSC "LatRailNet" (100%); LLC "LDZ Cargo Loģistika" (100%)	100	MoT	Transport	256 720 375	972 032 000	440 898 000	1 161 000	12 316
Eiropas dzelzceļa līnijas Subsidiaries: JSC "RB Rail" (33.3%)	100	MoT	Transport	680 000	680 000			
Namzinis	100	MoT	Real estate	113 777	56 749	454 410	22 561	30
Autotransporta direkcija	100	MoT	Transport	200 919	3 520 007	3 790 557	684 801	92

SOE name	% state-owned	Share-holder	Sector	Statutory capital (EUR)	Balance sheet total (EUR)	Net turnover (EUR)	Profit/losses (EUR)	Employ-ees
Latvijas autoceļu uzturētājs	100	MoT	Transport	35 186 323	62 967 433	63 843 290	1 540 191	1 368
Latvijas Pasts Subsidiaries: LLC "Mailmaster" (100%); JSC "IT Latvija" (78%); JSC "Latvijas pasta nodaļu tīkls" (80%)	100	MoT	Transport	10 578 515	94 434 778	61 685 223	1 727 197	4 204
Latvijas Valsts radio un televīzijas centrs Subsidiaries: LLC "Latvijas Mobilais Telefons" (23%)	100	MoT	Communi-cations	78 454 705	95 217 275	14 018 273	6 001 420	262
Latvijas Valsts ceļi	100	MoT	Transport	4 155 649	5 569 689	12 132 188	43 561	334
Latvijas gaisa satiksme	100	MoT	Transport	22 765 948	30 169 708	24 631 294	215 068	363
Starptautiskā lidosta "Rīga"	100	MoT	Transport	28 608 932	185 610 172	44 885 457	134 678	1 162
Latvijas Jūras administrācija	100	MoT	Transport	1 533 902	4 625 585	4 321 289	39 085	149
Ceļu satiksmes drošības direkcija Subsidiaries: LLC "Auteko & TÜV Latvija" (51%); LLC "Scantest" (20%); LLC "Venttests" (50%); LLC "Autests" (20%)	100	MoT	Transport	23 117 317	42 439 953	37 284 736	1 374 945	746
Pasažieru vilciens Subsidiaries: JSC "VRC Zasulauks" (51%)	100	MoT	Transport	20 868 047	36 251 698	62 278 754	-2 690 579	1 248
Air Baltic Corporation Subsidiaries: LLCA" Baltijas Kravu Centrs" (100%); LLC "Training Center Holding" (100%); LLC "Baltic Airlines" (100%); JSC "Aviation Crew Resources" (95.8%); LLC" Coalition Rewards" (96.4% owned by LLC" Baltic Airlines"); LLC "Air Baltic Training" (100% owned by LLC "Baltic Airlines"); LLC "Baltic Contact Centre" (100% owned by LLC "Baltic Airlines"); LLC "Travellounge" (100% owned by LLC "Baltic Airlines"); "Coalition Rewards" OOO (Russia) and "Coalition Rewards" oy (Finlanda) (100% owned by LLC "Coalition Rewards")	99.8	MoT	Transport	2 323 000	12 883 000	254 180 000	7 705 000	1 269
Šampētera nams	100	MoW	Real estate	230 816	470 160	711 905	-4 587	25
Latvijas radio Subsidiaries: Kurzemes radio (0.58%)	100	NEMMC	Media	824 685	7 666 475	9 176 443	147 877	255
Latvijas televīzija	100	NEMMC	Media	4 837 450	18 098 519	17 270 325	-132 941	453

1. VSIA Vides projekti has undergone insolvency procedures and was at the time of writing undergoing bankruptcy procedures.

2. *Note*: LPA = Latvian Privatisation Agency, MOA = Ministry of Agriculture, MOC = Ministry of Culture, MOE = Ministry of Energy, MoEPRD = Ministry of Environmental Protection and Regional Development, MoES = Ministry of Education and Science, MoF = Ministry of Finance, MOH = Ministry of Health, MOI = Ministry of Interior, MOJ = Ministry of Justice, MOT = Ministry of Transport, MOW = Ministry of Welfare, NEMMC = National Electronic Mass Media Council.

Source: Data provided by the Latvian authorities.

ORGANISATION FOR ECONOMIC CO-OPERATION AND DEVELOPMENT

The OECD is a unique forum where governments work together to address the economic, social and environmental challenges of globalisation. The OECD is also at the forefront of efforts to understand and to help governments respond to new developments and concerns, such as corporate governance, the information economy and the challenges of an ageing population. The Organisation provides a setting where governments can compare policy experiences, seek answers to common problems, identify good practice and work to co-ordinate domestic and international policies.

The OECD member countries are: Australia, Austria, Belgium, Canada, Chile, the Czech Republic, Denmark, Estonia, Finland, France, Germany, Greece, Hungary, Iceland, Ireland, Israel, Italy, Japan, Korea, Latvia, Luxembourg, Mexico, the Netherlands, New Zealand, Norway, Poland, Portugal, the Slovak Republic, Slovenia, Spain, Sweden, Switzerland, Turkey, the United Kingdom and the United States. The European Union takes part in the work of the OECD.

OECD Publishing disseminates widely the results of the Organisation's statistics gathering and research on economic, social and environmental issues, as well as the conventions, guidelines and standards agreed by its members.

OECD PUBLISHING, 2, rue André-Pascal, 75775 PARIS CEDEX 16
(26 2016 01 1 P) ISBN 978-92-64-26817-3 – 2017

www.ingramcontent.com/pod-product-compliance
Lightning Source LLC
Chambersburg PA
CBHW061220240926
51846CB00006B/1292
* 9 7 8 9 2 6 4 2 6 8 1 7 3 *